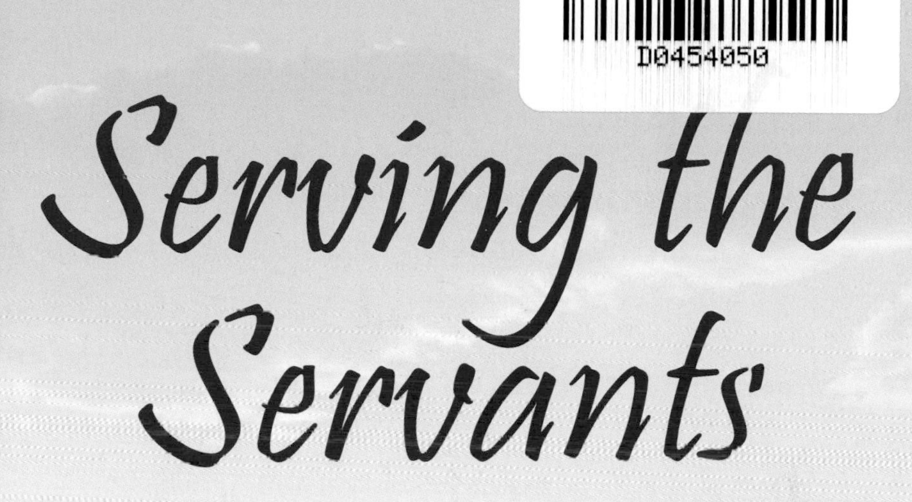

Serving the Servants

Ray Knighton

with

Phil Craven

A Founder's Reflections on the First 25 Years of MAP International

Published by BookEnd Publishing
One Cottonfield Road, Darien, GA 31305 USA
Phone 912.437.3770 Fax 912.437.4766

Printed in the United States of America.

ISBN 0-9703711-2-8

Library of Congress Control Number: 2001098458

To Beth,

my wife and sweetheart,

the mother of our children,

my best friend,
traveling companion,
and ministry partner,

without whom
none of this
would have been possible

Acknowledgements

So many people have contributed to the story of MAP International and to the events related in these pages that it would be impossible to name them all. To all those who might have been named here but are not, I apologize.

More than any other person, I owe a debt of gratitude to my wife, Elizabeth Reed Knighton. From the beginning, Beth has been my constant companion, counselor, co-worker, advisor and friend. I cannot imagine what life would be without her ever-faithful encouragement and support.

Amy Anderson, my secretary for much of MAP's history, was a dear friend to Beth and me, and a stand-in parent to our children when travel or other duties kept us away from our family. This book would not have been possible without Amy's diligence in collecting, collating, and preserving notes and itineraries, as well as other materials from our journeys. Amy has gone to be with the Lord, but to this book she has proven as indispensable in death as she was in life.

Many others made a significant contribution to the production of this volume. Bev Snedden, Beth's secretary for many years, produced an invaluable timeline of MAP's history. Dotsie Ross and Suzanne Baroody coordinated every aspect of production from concept to culmination. Sharon Bolin contributed sharp and incisive skills to the proofreading and copy editing of the manuscript. Michael Nyenhuis, MAP's current president, recognized the value of what we were doing and made sure that it remained a high priority within the organization.

Two longtime friends also contributed through publications of their own. Jim Hefley's book, *Intrigue in Santo Domingo*, and Viggo Olsen's autobiographical *Daktar: Diplomat in Bangladesh,* provided excellent accounts of events that greatly affected our lives and the life of MAP International. They were extremely helpful.

I am also indebted to the Robert Ruark archives at the University of North Carolina. Information from their encyclopedic collection of Ruark's papers provided answers I had long sought concerning Ruark's role in helping fund the fledgling Medical Assistance Programs.

For transcribing our memories and distilling them into the final form that appears here, my friend, Phil Craven must take a great deal of credit. Without him, this book would not have appeared for many years, if at all. I enjoyed our countless sessions of reminiscing, writing, and revising, but most of all, I enjoyed our fellowship as Christian brothers. Like so many who have served alongside me over the years, Phil's efforts have made me appear a better man than I ever felt myself to be.

Finally to the faithful servants of God who have staffed MAP's board, offices and distribution facilities down through the years, I am indebted beyond description. The accumulated mercies of their tireless efforts on behalf of the world's poor stand as a memorial worthy of all the servants of Christ who have gone before them. I pray God's blessing on each of them, and on all who follow after.

Ray Knighton
St. Simons Island, Georgia
2001

Foreword

Here is the fascinating inside story of the formation and development of one of the great missionary assistance programs of this generation. It is the story of the worldwide Medical Assistance Programs, better known as MAP, begun unexpectedly in the providence of God by Ray Knighton. He has written this book as a testimonial to the kindness of God in distributing lifesaving medicines to far-away missionary hospitals, where the message of eternal life is also proclaimed. Let us praise God together for using Ray to present this evidence of God's grace through His Church.

Kenneth N. Taylor, Litt.D.
President and Chairman of the Board,
Tyndale Publishing House and
Translator of *The Living Bible*

Introduction

Medicine is one of the original works of mercy and whether it is practiced under government, foreign agency, or missions, it is an expression of the Christian life. When it is practiced without superiority but with extreme skill and efficiency, and when it is practiced in love, the force of its impact is unquestioned.

I originally spoke those words at the first International Conference on Missionary Medicine at Wheaton College in the winter of 1959. That conference was the brainchild of J. Raymond Knighton, then executive director of the Christian Medical Society, and it brought together some 700 medical missions personnel from around the globe.

Those women and men were all engaged in a wide variety of health-related ministries, but they all shared a common purpose— to provide health for the world's poor, in Christ's name. They also shared another common link: a relationship with an organization known then as the Medical Assistance Programs of the Christian Medical Society.

In 1951 while studying for a graduate degree at Chicago Musical College in Chicago, Illinois, Ray Knighton became the part-time administrator for the fledgling Christian Medical Society. Later, Ray was named executive director for the national organization of the CMS when they took up residence in offices at 127 North Dearborn Street.

That year, in an incident detailed later in these pages, the pastor of my church in Philadelphia, Dr. Donald Grey

Barnhouse of Tenth Presbyterian Church, played a key role in having eleven tons of donated medical supplies delivered to the CMS offices. That donation provided the foundation for the formation of the Medical Assistance Programs of the Christian Medical Society.

With eleven tons of medical supplies threatening to burst the walls of his cramped office space, Ray Knighton faced the challenge of providing those supplies to medical missionaries serving overseas. Ray proved equal to the task and for the next twenty-six years, provided leadership to an agency that grew to become one of the world's leading Christian health organizations.

Through links with the CMS, Donald Grey Barnhouse, and the Christian community in Philadelphia, Ray and I have shared many experiences over the years. As a highly involved member of the CMS at the time the Medical Assistance Programs was constituted as a separate ministry, I played a key role in the founding of MAP. I continued to serve as a board member, leaving that post only when it was necessitated by my appointment as Surgeon General in 1981.

In some ways, I think of Ray as the brother I never had. I was an only child, and Ray and I share some remarkable similarities of appearance and experience, so much so that people on many occasions have asked whether we were, in fact, biological brothers. We are similar in physical size, we wear similar beards, and have both been engaged throughout our professional lives in differing aspects of medicine and missions.

In some of his qualities Ray has reminded me of Moses—a man who never sought a position of leadership, but was called by God into that role. In some ways he has reminded me of the Apostle Paul—a man who trained for one kind of profession, but was appointed by God to a servant's role in a different vocation which called upon him to minister, mentor, teach, and train.

More that forty-five years of continuous service to mankind from a heart dedicated to Christ and His Kingdom have yielded for Ray a remarkable list of awards and recognition including Knighthood in the Order of Christopher Columbus (Government of the Dominican Republic), Layman's Citation for Distinguished Service (American Medical Association),

Knight of the Great Band of Liberian Humane Order of African Redemption (Government of Liberia).

Over the years both Ray and his wife, Beth, have given themselves to be used by God for the encouragement and support of missionary health professionals as they have served in nearly two hundred nations of the world. Ray has often been quoted as saying, "We at MAP are the servants of the servants."

Ray, himself, has embodied a spirit of selfless servanthood throughout his career. More than one person has expressed the opinion that God gave Ray a body in proportion to the grand size of his heart. His service has always been characterized by those elements I enumerated earlier—skill, efficiency, and love given without condescension.

The significance of the element of love in medical ministry was highlighted for me by an incident that occurred in 1965 when I visited a number of countries in Africa along with Ray and Gus Hemwall, a fellow physician and MAP board member.

It was blazing hot under the African sun that day. The road we traveled boiled with thick dust behind the occasional passing lorry. Ray, Gus and I were walking toward town from a Christian hospital we had visited.

Ahead in the distance we saw an approaching figure, which seemed to be sliding along the ground. As the figure drew nearer, we recognized that it was a man whose legs had been shriveled by polio. He was making his way down the road on his hands and hips, reaching ahead, knuckles to the ground, lifting himself to swing his lower body forward. It looked like a slow and painful way to travel. When the man was close enough to speak we asked him where he was going.

"To the hospital," he replied.

Sympathizing with the obvious ordeal it was to move under his own power, we asked whether he realized that he had just passed a government-run hospital.

"Oh, yes," he said. "I know. But I'm going to the mission hospital. There, they love me."

In the pages that follow, the story unfolds of a remarkable career in international health ministry. This is the story of Ray and Beth Knighton, and the faithful dedication with which they have served the call of God through the work of MAP International.

But more than that, it is a story of the wonderful, sovereign power of God to accomplish great things with whatever gifts and abilities a person may have, if that person is fully committed to following the Lord wherever He may lead.

C. Everett Koop, M.D.
Former U.S. Surgeon General

Preface

During my years with MAP International I had numerous experiences that many people would define as "chance" or "luck." However, I have the assurance that the providential hand of God guided Beth and me, and others with whom we traveled to the remote corners of the earth.

The memories related in this volume come from my travels around the world during the first twenty-five years of MAP's existence. It should be noted that, for a greater understanding of my relationship with MAP, I have taken the liberty of relating incidents in my life prior to that time, and MAP's progress since.

These memoirs derive from a heart of gratitude for the opportunity to serve those physicians, nurses, and other health care personnel in the developing world who have sacrificed much to care for others in the name of Christ. They have enriched my life in many ways.

The French poet Charles Baudelaire wrote, "I have more memories than if I were a thousand years old." I can identify with his sentiments as I have reached deep into the recesses of my heart to relate the selected incidents here. The names and places are as accurate as I can recall; however, if an inaccuracy should be noted from time to time, please be assured that the intent of the stories is not compromised.

I trust that your reading of these experiences will touch your heart.

J. Raymond Knighton

Table of Contents

The Chapters

Ray Knighton poses in uniform at Camp Roberts army base, Paso Robles, California, 1943.

Chapter One

Sovereignty and Soldiering

Paso Robles, California, 1943

I may have been the only soldier in World War II whose life was saved by his big feet.

It was 1942 and I was a college sophomore. Together with some other fellows I signed up for what they called the Reserve Corps because the recruiting officer promised that if we signed up we'd be able to finish out our college programs before going into the service. I learned a lesson that many other young men have learned about the promises made by recruiting officers. Within a month or so we were all called up for active duty. In April 1943, I was sent to Fort Sheridan, north of Chicago, for training.

I may have been the most inept recruit the Army ever had. I flunked all the physical tests they gave me. I can't remember now whether I did it on purpose or not, but I didn't know what aspect of the service they were going to put me into, and it really didn't make any difference to me. Eventually, I was assigned to the Air Corps ground school and designated to be sent to Miami Beach where the Army had taken over a number of hotels for training.

When it came time for us to ship out I learned that I wouldn't be going with the others. My uniform wasn't complete. Army regulations stipulated that you had to have all your gear before you could be shipped out to your next duty station. But the Army didn't have any shoes to fit my size fourteen feet. Army policy also stated that if troops were held back for any reason, they were not shipped out later to catch up with their original group, but were sent to the next duty station receiving troops, no matter where it was.

So eventually, I was shipped to the infantry at Camp Roberts, in Paso Robles, California. I ended up in the desert as a foot soldier and went to work in a chapel as a volunteer with a Methodist chaplain, Claude Adams, playing the organ and singing in his services. Near the end of my training we had a forced march and I passed out because my feet were so bad, and ended up in the hospital. I was reclassified because of what they called hyper-mobile joints, which, as I understood it in layman's terms, meant I had no cushion in my walk. The doctors had determined that I was unfit for overseas service.

When that happened, Chaplain Adams put in a request for me to be permanently assigned as his assistant. He had been praying—and keeping a sharp lookout—for a permanent assistant. To him, I looked like a perfect candidate. When I went before the reclassification board they said they didn't have any positions specifically for musicians to assist chaplains, but they did have a position open for a clerk. They asked, "Can you type?" I said, "Yes." They didn't ask *how*, or how *fast*. I could only hunt-and-peck with two fingers, but it was typing, so I ended up as Chaplain Adams' assistant in June of 1943.

Being in the Chaplain Corps, Chaplain Adams—"Chappie," as we called him—had a pipeline into the head office so I knew that my first furlough was coming in October of 1943. Beth and I were already engaged at the time, so I talked to her and said "Why don't we go ahead and get married? You can come out here and live with me." So since I was one of the few guys who knew when my furlough was coming up, we were able to plan our wedding. And also, because I was in the Chaplain Corps, Chaplain Adams was able to get a reservation for me on an airplane—my very first airplane ride—to come back for the wedding.

We flew on United Airlines and it took 24 hours to fly from San Francisco to Chicago. We made seven stops, two of which were simply to take on fuel, but no passengers. I was the only enlisted man on the entire flight; all the rest were officers. So all the way back I didn't talk to anyone. It was torture to be so excited about going home for my wedding and not to be able to talk to anyone about it. But I didn't want anyone to know who I was or what I was doing, fearing that if anyone knew, somehow all our plans would be ruined.

So I got home and Beth and I were married on October 13, 1943. My parents gave us a railcar compartment ticket as a wedding gift, and we had our honeymoon on the train going back to California.

I spent the rest of the war at Camp Roberts in California and, in later years, sometimes told people that I fought the battle of "Guadaco-Roberts," which was my takeoff on the name Guadalcanal. Here again, I can look back and see the sovereignty and providence of God at work in my life. All the young men I trained with during my infantry time, many who were really just boys, were sent to Fort Ord. From there they were shipped out to a Pacific island called Guadalcanal. My fellow trainees were in the first wave of combat troops that landed on Guadalcanal and seventy-five percent were killed the first week of combat. But for the grace of God, that's where I would have been.

After the war, Beth and I came back to Chicago, and I finished my music degree at the American Conservatory of Music. The G.I. Bill enabled me to complete my music education through private lessons, and from there I was called to be the assistant pastor and music director at a Nazarene church in Lansing, Michigan. While I was in Lansing, I was able to attend Michigan State, and received my Masters in music in 1947. That same year I was called to be a professor of music at Northwest Nazarene College in Nampa, Idaho. So along with Beth and our first child, Nancye, I moved there in 1947 and taught music for three years. While we were there, our son David was born. We returned to Chicago in 1950 for me to do my Ph.D. in musicology, little realizing that the Lord was planning to change the direction of our lives through CMS, the Christian Medical Society.

Looking back on all of this now, I feel that a solid understanding of the sovereignty of God is the only way to get a grasp on the mystery of apparent circumstantial events that seem to direct our lives. It is very clear throughout the Bible that God knows exactly what is going to happen. Indeed, God directs the course of events to bring about His will for the lives of His people. Beth and I have seen it time and again, from the first day of MAP's existence. But perhaps nowhere is it clearer to me than in these events in which God providentially preserved my life, and positioned Beth and me to be used in the chain of events that resulted in the creation of an organization called MAP International.

Chapter Two

He Leadeth Me—
Early Life to the 50s

He leadeth me: O blessed thought!
O words with heav'nly comfort fraught!
What e'er I do, where'er I be,
Still 'tis God's hand that leadeth me.
—Joseph Gilmore

Chicago, Illinois, 1950

To me, the most significant illustration of God's grace has been my own experience. For example, I started out with no academic, professional, spiritual or physical qualifications for the job that I had for forty years—but God led me, and used me.

To start with, I didn't get a very good education in grade school or high school. It wasn't anyone's fault but my own. I just wasn't interested in studying. I *goofed off* for one entire year in high school because I believed that I was going to be a musician for the rest of my life. I could have been taking typing and other subjects that would have helped me later in my career. But I didn't think I needed those things. I had no idea that I would do anything but sing for the rest of my life.

But in His grace, God saw to it that I got to the places I was supposed to be. I can look back now and see that at every step, the Lord knew what He was doing, even though I *didn't* know what He was doing.

I vividly remember one evening in Chicago when I was doing my graduate work. I was walking from the El station back to our little place on the south side. As I walked I was saying, "Lord, how come I don't have any joy in what I'm doing?" I was walking down 63rd Street, passing by a pizza place. Pizza was a new thing in the neighborhood then, and I had no idea what pizza was. But I remember passing by that little place as I was saying, "Lord, I just don't have any peace. Why?" I didn't get a specific answer right then, but looking back, I can see that the Lord was causing me to be dissatisfied with where I was and what I was doing so that I'd be happy to do what He wanted me to do.

In 1950 a physician, Dr. Howard Hamlin, from my home church in Chicago, had been elected president of the Christian Medical Society (CMS). It was a Monday morning and Dr. Hamlin had just returned from a CMS convention in New York. Both of our children were ill that morning, and Howard came by on a house call.

"Ray, we don't have anyone who can run the CMS office for us," Howard said to me afterward. "Didn't you have some management and administration experience when you were teaching in Idaho?"

"A little bit," I replied.

"A little bit is all you need," Howard said. "Why don't you come down and run the office for me?"

"Howard, I'm really not interested," I said. And humanly speaking, I wasn't. But unknown to me, there were events taking place behind the scenes that would soon shape the course of my relationship with Howard and the CMS.

I had been teaching at the Chicago Evangelistic Institute, a Christian Bible college, and Howard was on the board of the school. I didn't know that the school was planning a move to Oskaloosa, Iowa. But Howard knew it—and he knew that I was soon going to be out of a job.

When I said, "Howard, I'm not interested." He insisted, "Ray, I'd really like to have you help me." We left it at that.

That night Howard and I were both attending a party for a young man from our church who was shipping out to the Korean War. As we were sampling items at the refreshment table Howard said, "Ray, I've made arrangements for you to go to Wheaton with me on Wednesday night to meet the executive committee of the CMS."

I said, "Howard, I told you I wasn't interested."

"Well, you can just ride out to Wheaton with me, can't you?" he said.

I said, "Yes. I'll do that—as a friend."

So that Wednesday night we went out to Wheaton. A former missionary to China, Dr. Paul Adolph, was the secretary of the executive committee. Paul had suffered a heart attack some time before, so the committee met at Paul's house so he wouldn't have to go out at night. I accompanied Howard to this executive committee meeting and that night they offered me a job.

I came on board for a month, part-time, at $75 per week. I wanted it to be part-time so I could do voice teaching on the side. That was actually the only formal arrangement I ever had with CMS or MAP. I never had a contract with the board, or any other agreement. I worked until 1980 on that basis. And it was never brought up. I was just *there*. My contract was simply an agreement with the Lord, an agreement that I would serve Him faithfully. I've tried to do that, but I suppose only in eternity will I really know how well I've done.

If that sounds overly humble, you have to remember that if you feel that you don't have anything to offer, then you don't have grounds for anything other than humility. And I had nothing to offer, other that a willing heart and a desire to help people, which I think I "inherited" from my mother.

Mom was always taking in *strays*, always caring for someone in our home, helping them along to regain their health, or their confidence, or whatever it was they had lost. This was just her nature, and I grew up with these people sharing food at our table all the time. Usually, I had no idea who these people were, but Mom was looking after them. She didn't make any special effort to instill her sense of service in us, but from her example we learned to help people who were hurting.

Her father was the same way, and he had a big influence on me as I was growing up. Grandpa Anderson was a very outgoing man who was the spiritual leader in our family and in our church. The offering used to be taken up in a very public manner at our church, and they were often seeking a specific amount from the congregation. Granddad would stand up and say, "I'll give the last hundred dollars. You all put in the rest and I'll give the last hundred." He was always the most generous man in the church.

To his dying day, Grandpa Anderson's children had to keep him supplied with money to give away because he had long since given away all of his own money. But all through the Depression, Grandpa Anderson always had a job, and always had something to give to those in need. There were some lean times when my parents didn't even have enough money for food at suppertime. After school in those days I would get on the streetcar at 63rd Street, pay three cents, and ride for half an hour to Stewart Avenue, then walk about a block to Grandpa's house for supper. My folks would meet me there for the evening meal. We did that for two or three years.

Growing up with spiritual influences like that, it's perhaps no surprise that my conversion experience was more an ongoing process than a singular event. Our church used to put on tent meetings in a vacant lot a few blocks from my house. I went every night to sing in the choir.

One evening the preacher was a woman named Stella Crooks. I was a senior in high school at that time. When she gave the invitation I went forward, and I look back on that now as the beginning of my commitment to Christ. I don't think it was instantaneous at the time, but I began to grow spiritually, and as I grew, there were several experiences of God's grace being poured out on me. It was a defining moment for me, but from the Lord's perspective, I think it was merely a step along the road where He was leading me.

By leading me into my role with CMS, and later with MAP, the Lord thrust me into the position of a spiritual leader to the people serving with me in the organization. I admit that I often felt very inadequate. I knew very well that I needed spiritual guidance myself.

I did a lot of counseling in those days, but it was always with a sense of my own neediness and dependence on God. One young lady, now named Phyllis Irwin, was a medical student at the University of Indiana and planning on going to the mission field. After I spoke at her CMS group, Phyllis asked if we could talk.

"Ray," she said, "I feel definitely called to the mission field with the Methodist Church. And they are paying some of the expenses for my medical training. But I've fallen in love with a fellow attending Grace Seminary and he is not a Methodist. I think he might be the farthest thing from a Methodist, theologically. What am I going to do?"

I said, "Phyllis, there are many mission boards, other than denominational boards, that would be thrilled to have both you and this young man." I began telling her about a number of missions where she, with her Methodist background, and Russ, with his Baptist background, could serve together because the missions weren't structured along denominational lines.

When I mentioned TEAM (The Evangelical Alliance Mission) Phyllis said, "That sounds like the one for me!" Evidently she was right. She and her husband spent some forty years in Pakistan at the Bach Missionary Hospital in the Hazarajab area north of Islamabad.

Time and again throughout my life and my ministry with MAP, I've seen similar examples of God's providence and sovereignty at work. My own experience of confirmation that I was called into this type of ministry is another example.

I was in Philadelphia to speak to a group of graduate physicians who were members of CMS. They met in the Drexel Hill area, in the home of Dr. Balian.

After the meeting a man approached who was a surgeon in Philadelphia. He just looked at me and said, "You're our 'Stacey Woods,' aren't you?" This was Dr. J. Winslow Smith, and we were to become very good friends in the years ahead.

He was referring to the man who had brought the ministry of InterVarsity Christian Fellowship (IVCF) to the U.S. from England. In my mind, Stacy Woods was a spiritual giant. "I'm afraid I'm anything but a 'Stacey Woods,'" I replied. But at that moment, I felt for the first time a sense of conviction that said, "Lord, I'm here because You have put me here." And that confirmed in my heart and mind that I should be with CMS at that time. I still believe that strongly.

God has shown me many times that I am not in charge, but He is. On trips overseas, sometimes I would have to spend all day in an airport waiting for the weather to change or some other difficulty to clear up. There was, for example, the time we were trying to get from Raxall to New Delhi. We were supposed to go through Katmandu but nothing was on time, and nothing went as planned all day. I learned that you just have to say, "Okay, God. You have a plan for us that involves being late for our reception in New Delhi." If it weren't for that assurance, I don't think I would have been able to keep my sanity, especially traveling at that time when we didn't have all the conveniences we have today.

The assurance that God has a plan has extended to every area of our journey with MAP. Over the years people have often asked about my vision for MAP. I've had to say that honestly, my vision usually extended no farther than the end of the day. I just tried to get through the day's demands and harbored no illusions that I had any idea what tomorrow would bring. My vision, if you can call it that, was simply to please God that day. That's really all a believer can do because God hasn't promised tomorrow to anyone.

I'll always remember something that was said to me by Dr. Jack Hough, chairman of MAP's board for many years: "Tomorrow *isn't*. Yesterday is *past*. All we have is *today* and that's why it's called the *present*, because it is a present, a gift from God." So I have always tried to take one day at a time. You never know how significant the events of a single day may be, but one day in 1954, I would learn.

Chapter Three

In the Beginning

Chicago, Illinois, 1954

From my point of view, the ministry of MAP International began one day in April 1954.

At that time the Christian Medical Society (CMS) offices consisted of one room, about thirty feet square, on the fifth floor of a dilapidated office building in downtown Chicago, a building which has long since been demolished.

We were there because the rent was cheap, and it was cheap for reasons that became quite clear if you were there for any amount of time. We often said that we rarely lost any item of our office supplies while there because the floors were so badly slanted that anything you dropped immediately rolled to one side of the room. If you ever lost anything, you could usually just walk over on the other side and pick it up.

Our staff consisted of a secretary, a bookkeeper, a clerk, and me—the four of us. At that time I spent about seventy percent of my time traveling for CMS, starting Bible study groups on various medical school campuses, and editing our CMS journal. For many people it will be hard to imagine me as a magazine editor since I have a difficult time spelling even the simplest words, but that's what I did.

One day I received a phone call at the office. It was from a man named Art Larson. I'll never forget Art, and I can picture him clearly now in my mind's eye because some years later I had the privilege of meeting him in person.

Art's call that day was to this effect: "I attend a Bible class in New York that meets every Monday night. Dr. Donald Gray Barnhouse from the Tenth Presbyterian Church in Philadelphia comes to New York every Monday night to teach the class.

I'm also an executive with Schering Drug Company and I have often heard in church about the great needs for medicine among medical missionaries. When I heard through our company grapevine that we were throwing away about $26,000 worth of usable medicines, I went to Dr. Barnhouse and asked whether there wasn't some way to get these into the hands of medical missionaries."

Now Dr. Barnhouse was a great man, with a great big voice, and I can almost hear him replying to Art in his booming voice: "Well, sir, I know a man who knows every medical missionary in the world. Send the medicines to him."

Apparently Dr. Barnhouse had our name and address right there with him, and Art was led to believe that we had a program of sending surplus medicines to medical missionaries. Of course, at that time, we had never thought of it.

Somewhat cautiously I replied to Art, "Yes, we do have contact with two or three hundred medical missionaries who are part of the CMS."

"Wonderful," Art said. "I've just shipped you eleven tons of medicines."

In shock I gasped, "You did what?"

In later years, people often stopped me when I was leading tours of a well-stocked distribution center and said, "It must be wonderful to reflect on the great vision you saw of a way to help needy people around the world and how it has all come to pass." And I would think: "If you only knew the thoughts I had when that first shipment arrived!" I had no idea how we would manage to distribute the medicines that arrived in that first donation.

I'm sure that if Art had called up and asked whether he could ship the medicines, I would have said, "No way. We have no where to put them." And it was true. We didn't even have a closet in our little office space. What few supplies we could afford were stacked on a small metal shelf over in the corner of the room—the corner everything rolled to.

But this is the way God works. He knew how I acted—and reacted—so He arranged it in a way that kept me from spoiling it. A few days later I got a call from a trucking company wanting to know where our warehouse was. I had to laugh. Then I said we're at 128 N. Dearborn. (If you look up that address now, you won't find our building. It's where the famous Picasso sculpture now stands.)

He said, "What!" In those days, the truckers had to get special permission to bring a truck like that into downtown Chicago during business hours. But he arrived the next day with a truck carrying eleven tons of medicines.

As I said, there were four of us on staff, just three ladies and myself. So, it was left to me to unload the truck. We didn't even have a hand truck, since we obviously had no need for one.

So before I could unload the truck I went to the stationery store across the street and bought a two-wheeled hand truck for $6.95. Then I unloaded 11 tons of medicines.

There was no freight elevator in our building, just one small passenger elevator. It took me over 8 hours going up and down in this little elevator which was stuffed with passengers on nearly every trip.

On one of these trips in the elevator Dr. A.W. Tozer, the great Christian and Missionary Alliance pastor, was a passenger. Dr. Tozer was on his way up to the second floor for a noonday service that was held there. "What in the world are you doing, Ray?" he asked. All I could think to say was, "Don't ask."

I was not happy. We pushed all the desks to one side and stacked eleven tons of medicine on the floor. I was sure the load was going to cave through the floor and smash down to the first level. Two or three days later we found some other space in the building and again I took eleven tons of medicine down to the new location on the same elevator.

Of course, as I could clearly see later, God was superintending everything. It was a blessing that the American Medical Association (AMA) was having its annual meeting in

Chicago that year. I knew that a lot of missionaries would be coming to the convention. So I spread the word in a letter to everyone I knew who might be driving in for the convention from five or six hundred miles around. In the letter I told them what we had on hand and said, "If it would please you, we would love for you to get this out of here so we can get back to work."

And they took it all. We have no record now of the recipients of the first shipment of supplies from MAP because it all went out with those missionaries. When it was gone, we all breathed a sigh of relief that the episode was over. Or so we thought.

Just about that time I received a letter from Dr. Sheila Gupta, an Indian national and a Christian physician, reporting that there was a polio epidemic. She had read in *TIME Magazine* that the Salk polio vaccine was just on the market and was wondering if we could get 1,000 doses of the vaccine for use in her clinic.

My first inclination—and I came very close to doing it—was to dictate a nice letter saying that we were very sorry but we just did not have the time or personnel needed to get involved in that sort of effort. Instead, I pushed the letter around on my desk for a week. I suppose I was subconsciously hoping that it would fall into the wastebasket. I didn't want to handle it.

But my conscience kept bothering me. Finally, I decided I had to make an effort, no matter how small. At least that way I could be turned down and legitimately report that I had tried but failed.

I checked with a friend and found that there were six companies making the polio vaccine. One of them was Eli Lilly, based nearby in Indianapolis. I had an acquaintance there, a physician on Lilly's staff named Dudley Dennison, who was a member of CMS.

I called Dudley who said, "Yes, we're making the vaccine, but I'm in research. However, if you want to come down here for a visit, I can get you an interview with someone who can tell you all about it."

So I did. I took the train to Indianapolis and ended up in a very posh office. I have to admit that I didn't look at the door when I was shown in and didn't realize until later that I was with the president of the company.

After the pleasantries of being introduced, I showed him the letter I'd gotten from India.

"Well, we can't sell any of this," he said. "This is absolutely not for sale. For the next few weeks, months, probably years all the Salk polio vaccine we can make is going to city and county public health services to immunize the entire population of children in the United States."

"I suppose it's good that you can't sell it," I said. "I don't have any money to buy it."

But then he said, "We're making about 3 million doses per day. A thousand wouldn't be missed, would it?"

I said, "I guess not." And he said, "We'll give you a thousand doses. But it has to stay cold. It must remain frozen. Do you have any facilities for packing it in dry ice?"

I said that we didn't.

He said, "Well, I suppose we could pack it for you. Do you think you could ship it?" And I said, "Yes, I think we can make arrangements to get it there." And we did make arrangements to have it transported via Pan Am airlines, which allowed the medicines to be hand-carried by the cockpit crew from Chicago, to New York, to Europe, and on to Bombay.

While we were talking the president of Lilly said, "You know Mr. Knighton, we'd love to be able to help medical missionaries, but we have no one we can trust to get the material to them. About two years ago we sent $10,000 worth of supplies right off our shelves here to a hospital in Taegu, Korea. But it never arrived. Somewhere along the line it was stolen or diverted and was on the black market when we found it. Obviously, we can't have that. But if we could find someone we could trust we would love to help. Might you be that someone?"

Of course, I knew the hospital he was speaking of, and knew Howard Moffat, the medical director there. So I knew we might provide the link he was looking for. I said, "Yes, I might be that someone."

So he invited me to stay for lunch. During lunchtime he had the legal department draw up an affidavit stating that I would personally be responsible for everything that Eli Lilly gave to the CMS at the time. To my knowledge, that document is still on file at the company headquarters.

This was June of 1954. By August of that year I had met a researcher who worked for the Upjohn Company in Kalamazoo, Michigan and attended the Christian Reformed Church there. He said, "Hey, I think this is a great idea. It seems like we always have some medicines or supplies that are usable, but not suitable for sale. We would love for someone to be able to use them in medical missions."

Soon we began receiving supplies from Upjohn. One thing led to another and before long, the Medical Assistance Programs of the Christian Medical Society was up and running.

Chapter Four

The Man God Uses

Wheaton, Illinois, 1959

It was Christmastime 1959, and Pierce Chapel, on the campus of Wheaton College, was crowded with some 700 doctors, nurses, students, and missionaries from around the world. As usual for Wheaton at that time of year, the ground outside was blanketed with snow. But inside, the speaker addressing this diverse assembly of medical personnel was just beginning to warm up.

"If you'll look at the roster of the spiritually successful—Abraham, Job, David, Paul, St. Francis, Chrysostom, Luther, Augustine, Livingstone and all the rest, this was their secret: 'Be Thou exalted, O God, over me. Have first place, God. Be Thou exalted over me, O God. Exalt Thyself at my expense. At any cost, be Thou exalted, O God.' Somebody said with eschatological soundness, 'My kingdom go' is the necessary corollary of 'Thy kingdom come.' And until my kingdom goes, His kingdom can't come."

Dr. A. W. Tozer was a well-known minister in the Christian and Missionary Alliance, editor of *Alliance Witness* and author of numerous books including *The Pursuit of God*. Dr. Tozer was the devotional speaker for the first International Conference on Missionary Medicine (ICMM).

Tozer had chosen as his theme, "The Man God Uses." Today we might feel the need for a more inclusive title, but the women and men packing that chapel in 1959 had no doubt that Tozer's message was truly inclusive in the deepest sense. His remarks were aimed at the heart of each and every one of us.

As I sat there with the others, listening to Dr. Tozer's message, I took deep satisfaction from the fulfillment of a dream that had started two years earlier with the remark of a student to me at the InterVarsity Missionary Conference in Urbana, Illinois. A couple of thousand of Christian students from around the country had come together for a conference highlighting the needs and opportunities in world missions. One of the medical students in attendance said to me, "Ray, this is a great conference, but there's really nothing here for *us.*"

I knew exactly who was meant by "us," and she was right; the conference didn't present a specific track for those interested in medical missions. The idea immediately began forming in my mind for MAP to host an international conference on missionary medicine that would bring health practitioners from all over the world to a place where they could share ideas and needs, and find answers and resources, to help in the specialized ministries to which God had called them.

Although the idea for this conference was just beginning to form in my mind, God was already at work putting in place the people we would need to make it happen. We had no idea how to orchestrate such a conference, but I remembered a conversation with a young woman named Amy Anderson who had told us about organizing the first conference for Billy Graham in Europe for Youth for Christ (YFC). So in 1959 we hired Amy to come to CMS and organize the first ICMM for us.

Amy began her secretarial career working for the government, but she soon went to work for Torrey Johnson, the evangelist. Torrey had founded YFC and Amy was one of the first employees of that ministry.

At one time she had two young evangelists for whom it was her responsibility to get preaching assignments: Bob Pierce, founder of World Vision, and Billy Graham. Amy worked for YFC for many years, and Billy later told me that Amy was a tremendous help at the YFC office. "We were very blessed to have Amy working with us those years," he said. One of her most important contributions was setting up YFC's first conference in Europe. Later, she went to work for Dr. Gus Hemwall, and that was where we met her.

From the first day Amy took it on herself to look after me completely. For example, I never had to dictate a letter for Amy; she wrote all my letters for me. I'd sit down with Amy and a pile of correspondence and say things like, "Okay, here's a letter from Dr. Koop. You know how well I know Chick. Send him a reply and tell him, 'yes,' I'll do what he's asking." Then I'd just hand her the letter and she would come up with an excellent reply. They were so well composed you'd think I had spent an hour dictating them.

Amy did this so well that one time she embarrassed me. She always opened my mail and one time, while I was traveling, I got a letter from a Baptist missionary from Paraguay whose son had drowned. She knew how well I knew him, so before I got back she had written him a nice letter that ministered to him and signed my name to it.

By the time I got back from my trip I had on my desk the original letter, my reply to it via Amy, and his letter of reply to me, telling me how wonderful my letter was and how much he appreciated my taking the time to think of him.

I took the three letters to Amy and said, "Amy! This makes me feel terrible! This fellow is heaping praises on me, and I didn't even know about the terrible tragedy he had suffered!"

Amy said, "Calm down, Ray. It's all right. God has assigned me to be your voice and when you're gone, I do your work. I knew what you would write if you had been here, so I wrote it." I said, "Amy, I wouldn't have done it as well as you did."

Over the years, Amy became so close to our family that she even helped raise our kids. When they were in school, if Beth had to go with me to a convention, Amy would move into the house while we were away. The kids loved it when "Aunt Amy" came because she spoiled them and let them eat whatever they wanted. Amy's brother, Carl, was a banker in nearby Barrington, and her sister-in-law, Anne, was an excellent volunteer executive secretary for Beth for many years. But other than Carl and Anne, Amy had no immediate family, so we became her family. Our kids were her kids.

Despite all her exemplary qualities, everyone didn't always appreciate Amy. She was very tenacious and her confidence, ingenuity, and loyalty were remarkable.

I remember one time in the late 60s when we were planning a conference. Thinking out loud I said, "Wouldn't it be great if we could get John Glenn to speak?" As America's first man in space, Glenn was an unparalleled hero at the time and a celebrity of first rank. "Of course, we would never be able to get hold of him," I said.

"Why not?" Amy asked.

"I'm sure Mr. Glenn has far too many demands on his time right now," I said. "We'd never be able to get through to him."

A few days later, Amy came into my office and said, "Ray, I've got John Glenn on the phone. Would you like to speak to him?"

After I got my lower jaw up off the floor, I spoke with Mr. Glenn and even though he was very interested in our conference, previous commitments prevented him from being involved. I was shocked, but looking back on it, I'm sure I shouldn't have been. That was typical of Amy—confident, resourceful, and full of ingenuity.

Amy's love for people and her love for God were the two qualities that most impressed Beth and me. Amy was one of the most selfless people we had ever met. She also loved her work and felt that God had called her to her job. As a result, there was no limit to the amount of time and effort she would put into it. She often came to work at seven or seven-thirty in the morning and stayed until ten or eleven at night.

Perhaps Amy could best be characterized by two small details that stand out in my mind. First, Amy had the checks for her checking account personalized by having them inscribed with a line from Philippians 1:21: "For me, to live is Christ." Second, the radio dial in Amy's car was permanently stuck on the Chicago-area Christian radio station, WMBI. When our son-in-law, Brad, bought the car from Amy, he came in and said, "The radio is stuck! It won't pick up any station except

WMBI." I said, "Brad, maybe this is the Lord's way of getting you to hear more of His word." Rather than replace the radio, Brad just listened to WMBI whenever he was driving.

When Amy retired from MAP after twenty years of service, the board gave her an around-the-world trip so she could visit many of the hospitals and missionaries she had served so faithfully. Amy has since gone to be with the Lord, but her contribution to MAP continues. This book is largely made possible by eight volumes of letters, itineraries, trip journals and photos that Amy collected over the years.

Without Amy's help, I believe it would have been impossible for us to organize a conference like the ICMM, where health practitioners from all over the world could network among themselves to find the resources to help in their specialized ministries.

An example of this type of networking occurred one day during lunchtime as I was patrolling the tables in the upper room of Wheaton College's old dining hall. A missionary physician who was serving in Africa caught my attention and waved me over to his table.

"I wonder if you can help me, Ray," he said. "I really need a fellow physician who is current in the latest surgical techniques to come over and help me learn some advanced urological procedures. I see a lot of such cases, and I need more training and the equipment to do it."

I made a mental note of it and all during lunch as I circled among the tables I kept an ear open for someone who could help.

As Ralph Blocksma would later describe it, the conference was like a day in the marketplace in a developing country. A place where health and medical personnel from around the globe could come to swap stories, trade ideas, and share solutions to the common challenges they faced. In doing so, all would be strengthened and encouraged to go back to their place of service and make a difference in the world around them.

Ralph had taken the podium for the keynote address at the opening of the conference. "I am going to say things to you that are disturbing, and with some of these comments you are perhaps going to take violent exception," he had said. "But if I create in your mind a deep desire for basic, honest research into the colossal problems facing us in the field of medical missions today, then I have been successful."

Coming from a man who is one of the greatest encouragers I know and whose message was perhaps the most lovingly presented of any at the conference, this was a bit incongruous.

Ralph went on to say, "Recently a professor from a Christian college in Pakistan made a shocking statement in my home. He said, 'The greatest moment in the history of the Christian Church in Pakistan will be the day the last foreign missionary leaves our soil.'"

While his words might have seemed a bit inflammatory, the professor was simply trying to make the point that for Christian missionaries to minister effectively in Pakistan they would have to go forth not as "lords and masters," Ralph said, but as "humble servants intent on representing ourselves solely as fellow Christians determined only to serve."

This emphasis on a humble desire to serve resurfaced again and again throughout the conference.

In a later address to the conference, Dr. L. Nelson Bell, the founding editor of *Christianity Today*, a pioneer medical missionary in China and the father of Ruth Bell Graham, emphasized that the character required for medical missions was one of humility and conscious dependence on God.

"Today we are intrigued with outer space, with the splitting of the atom, and all the things that have come along with that," the grandfatherly Southern gentleman said. "We are prone to think that these things have been created by man. Actually, man has never discovered anything other than what God put there in the first place, and power belongs to God. Aside from the presence and the power of Christ, nothing can be done that will last for eternity."

I couldn't have better orchestrated such thematic unity if I had dictated the content of each speaker's presentation myself. "In this conference, we are principally interested in the individual," Ralph had said. "We would like to know where you as a Christian personality fit into the whole picture. Are you the man or woman that God uses?"

If repetition is the soul of good teaching, then it was clear to me that the Lord had guided each speaker so that the point was repeatedly made as to the character and quality needed in the people God uses.

As technical advisor to the American Leprosy Missions and president of the Christian Medical Fellowship of Great Britain, another of our speakers, Bob Cochrane, was a recognized authority who had devoted a lifetime to ministry to people afflicted with disease.

"It seems to me," Bob said, "quite apart from general principles, that medical work should be an example of Christ's compassion to the non-Christian world. Even without a mission hospital, the ministry of healing, in the New Testament sense, could still be used by the Church as a powerful factor in the restoration of health.

"The Christian Church through the medical missionary enterprise has led the way in many lands for the compassionate care of the sick and suffering, and has stimulated a sense of responsibility in nations which are not Christian to take an active part in the relief of suffering. It can be maintained that the work of missionaries has paved the way to an entirely new approach to medicine.

Dr. C. Everett Koop, a future Surgeon General of the United States who, at that time, was fast becoming a world-renowned pediatric surgeon, echoed the need for Christian health practitioners to exhibit the highest character qualities.

"Medicine is one of the original works of mercy," Koop said. "And whether it be practiced under government, foreign agency, or missions, it is an expression of the Christian life. When it is practiced without superiority but with extreme skill and efficiency, and when it is practiced in love, the force of its impact is unquestioned. When those qualities are present in the life and work of any woman or man of God, they are attractive, and compelling. An attractive, competent Christian, one who is expert in his field, is one of the best advertisements for Christianity."

An incident that occurred a year and a half earlier validated what Koop was saying.

I had received a call from the dean of the University of Afghanistan School of Medicine. Afghanistan was perhaps one of the countries in the world most resistant to Christian missions at that time. But this Afghan University dean called to inquire whether the Christian Medical Society could supply two teachers for their medical school. I warned him in correspondence that these men would be Christians. He said, "We realize that. That's why we came to you."

Clearly, this Afghan dean had seen something in Christian believers that was attractive enough to outweigh any concern he had about such people teaching in his university. In his final devotional message to the conference, Dr. Tozer said that the secret to such attractive Christianity was found in something beyond techniques and methods.

"It is my conviction that unlovely Christianity has done more to turn away people from Christ than all the error in the world," A.W. Tozer was saying. "The answer is not in techniques or methods. The answer is the fire of the Holy Ghost burning in the heart of a man. This is the world's sundown, and there are men looking for somebody who looks like God. Someone, somewhere, is looking in your direction."

About fifteen minutes after my lunchroom conversation with the Africa-based physician who was looking for a urologist to help him I encountered just such a physician from Billings, Montana. I can't recall the fellow's name now, but I remember telling him about my conversation with the missionary physician from Africa. This fellow immediately responded, "I'd love to do that."

I hurried back to the table where I had met the missionary and he was still there finishing his lunch. Delighted that he hadn't left yet, I said, "Wait right here. Don't move. I'm going to get the answer to your prayer."

I located my urologist friend and introduced the two men. Within the year, the physician from Billings and the missionary in Africa were together on the field: one receiving the continuing education he needed, the other receiving a blessing that really can't be measured—the opportunity to see firsthand the profound impact of medical missions.

MAP's triennial missions conferences continued up until 1996, when the last one was held at a retreat center on St. Simons Island, Georgia. I always felt that this particular incident was typical of the success we had with the marketplace idea for these conferences, and for many years it was an excellent forum for matching up missionary needs with medical resources.

Endnote: In 1978 MAP instituted the Ralph Blocksma Award, which was given during MAP's missions conferences to recognize individuals who had offered exemplary, dedicated, compassionate medical service to the world's poor in Christ's name. The list of Blocksma Award winners includes:

1978 Denis Burkitt, M.D., F.A.C.S.
1981 Paul W. Brand, C.B.E., M.B.B.S., F.R.C.S., F.A.C.S.
Margaret Brand, M.B.B.S.
1984 Kenneth M. Scott, M.D., F.A.C.S.
1987 William J. Barnett, M.D.
1990 Hans L. E. Gruber, M.D., M.Sc., F.R.C. Path.
1993 J. Raymond Knighton, LL.D.
1996 Jose Miguel D'Angulo, M.D.

Dr. C. Everett Koop, (former US surgeon general) in conference at MAP's headquarters in Brunswick, Georgia, 1986.

Chapter Five

Travels with "Chick" and Gus

Africa, 1961

It's hard to imagine two men who could be more different from each other than Gustav A. Hemwall and C. Everett Koop.

Koop was an Eastern city boy from an erudite background. His father was a banker in New York. "Chick," as we called him, held prestigious positions as a pediatric surgeon at the University of Pennsylvania and surgeon-in-chief at Children's Hospital, University of Pennsylvania. Gus was the son of Swedish immigrants and a general practitioner who performed general surgery and did obstetrics.

In 1961, just after Belgian Congo was made independent, we received a call from three physicians there—Drs. Warren and Gretchen Berggren and Dr. Glen Tuttle. Practically all the medical facilities in Congo were critically short of personnel and supplies. Together with Warren, Gretchen, and Glen a number of missionary physicians in that central African country were asking MAP for help. Our response was to set up the Congo Protestant Relief Agency (CPRA). I arranged a visit to help organize this new consortium. A good friend, Dr. Els Culver, then the executive vice president at World Vision, had arranged a grant of two thousand dollars to cover the expenses.

Not being a physician, I was not an expert in medical matters. Unbeknownst to me—or to each other—both "Chick" and Gus were planning to go along as my medical advisors. When I learned about their plans, I said to Beth, "I don't know if this is going to work. No two guys that I know are more different than Hemwall and Koop." But both were good personal friends and very strong supporters of CMS and MAP, and I couldn't turn either one of them down.

Our first stop was London where we met with Dr. Douglas Johnson, then the executive director of the Christian Medical Fellowship of Great Britain. I had remarked to my companions that while in London I wanted to meet Dr. Martin Lloyd Jones who had served as minister of Westminster Chapel for twenty-five years and was an internationally recognized and respected preacher. I was hoping to invite him to speak at MAP's International Conference on Missionary Medicine, which had become a triennial gathering of medical workers from all around the world.

We had heard that Dr. Jones was so busy that the only way to see him was to attend his Friday night Bible study. Afterwards, Dr. Jones hosted a reception for visitors from outside the country. We arrived at the church on a cold Friday night in January, expecting to meet in the church basement with half a dozen people. We were amazed to see a thousand people, most of them young women and men, gathered in the sanctuary for Bible study.

We took our seats and suddenly, out of the narthex of the church, there appeared this little old man who proceeded to climb up into the church's very high pulpit. This was Dr. Jones, who commenced his teaching by saying, "As you know we have been studying the Book of Romans for some years now. We've been in chapter ten for three weeks, and I hope tonight we'll finish verse nine." We were in for a treat.

Dr. Jones began to speak and it was absolutely captivating. He went on and on, expounding on the depth of meaning in this one verse. It was one of the most inspiring things I've ever heard in my life. Koop leaned over to me and said, "Where are we going to be next Friday night? We've got to come back and hear the end of this verse."

"We'll be in Egypt," I said.

After the service we were introduced to Dr. Jones, and I was blessed to encounter him again on a number of occasions after that. Although he was very interested in speaking at one of our conferences, much to my disappointment, the timing never worked out.

While in England, we also spent an evening with Dr. Roy Shaffer and his family. Roy, the son of pioneering missionaries, had grown up in Africa and later directed training programs through MAP's office in East Africa. Roy was very impatient with the provincial attitudes that some missionaries exhibited toward the nationals.

One group of medical missionaries, when asked by Dr. Johnson about plans to nationalize the hospital, had replied, "Never. These guys (the Africans) will never be able to take care of things once these facilities are nationalized." Dr. Koop was also very upset with that kind of thinking. Nationalization of the hospitals was necessary and inevitable, but Koop insisted that many, at that time, just couldn't see the big picture.

From London we traveled to Egypt, to the American hospital where Dr. Paul Jameson served as the physician. We passed through Cairo and spent the night at the hospital in Tanta. The next morning I asked Gus, "How did you sleep?"

"I slept pretty well," Gus said. "But I had the craziest dream. All night long I kept seeing these dancing bears from a television commercial." When Gus began humming the tune he'd heard in his dream I immediately recognized it and knew why he'd had such a bizarre dream. While he was sleeping, Gus was hearing the call to prayer from the local mosque. Oddly enough, it was basically the same tune as a popular American beer commercial.

That afternoon, we were sitting in a meeting with Chick and Gus and Paul and some Egyptian Christian physicians. In the Arab world, as soon as you sit down they immediately bring you a cup of Turkish coffee. This is a type of powdered coffee loaded with sugar and burned in the bottom of a pan. I think it is just about the most highly concentrated coffee you'll find anywhere.

Now the three of us had made an agreement that as we were meeting with various people on this trip that we would all eat or drink whatever was put in front of us. Generally, Gus never drank anything other than water, and I doubt whether he ever drank more than two cups of coffee a year.

I was feeling playful, so I leaned over to Gus and said, "If you drink it down all at once, it's easier." Of course, that is *not* the way you do it. Well, Gus was going along with our agreement and he downed the whole thing. It was like a straight shot of highly concentrated caffeine. Gus later said that his heart went into fibrillation, the hair on his neck and arms stood up, and he thought he was going to have a heart attack right there.

Of course, as soon as you drink it down, a servant shows up and fills it up again, so Gus was pretty unhappy with me. For many years afterward, whenever we were out to dinner together, I would say, "Gus, drink it all at once." He always laughed but said, "Every time you say that I go into the same reaction."

At one missionary hospital in Ethiopia I witnessed something that has always stayed with me. Dennis Carlson, the physician there, was treating an old, white-haired man in the hospital clinic. Dennis had arrived in the country fairly recently and had not had much language training. He was having a very difficult time communicating with this gentleman.

I was sitting there watching when suddenly, Dennis went over to the door and called his five-year-old son in. He told his son, "Ask this old 'Babba' this question." And Dennis told his son in very simple English what to ask. Then the boy repeated the question to the old man in his own language. I thought it was remarkable that this boy, who had quickly learned the language from playing with the local children, was able to communicate with an Ethiopian five or ten times his age so his dad could treat him with the proper medicine.

From Ethiopia we traveled to Nairobi, and from Nairobi to Dar Es Salaam, Tanzania. Then in Dar Es Salaam, after East Africa, we split up. Chick went to Johannesburg, South Africa and Gus went to Southern Rhodesia to be with Al Clemenger who was a missionary doctor there with TEAM. Al used to work with Gus in Oak Park. Then I met up with Gus in Johannesburg and so did Koop.

On our way back from South Africa, we went to the Congo where our host was Dr. Bill Rule, a physician with the Southern Presbyterian mission. Congo had just become independent, and there was a fair amount of unrest as the leaders figured out how to govern. The three of us were traveling a jungle road with Bill and his driver when we were stopped by a roadblock of Congolese troops. Bill spoke to the guard and then returned to our vehicle with a question.

"The guard says we need a 'laissez-passer'" Bill reported. I'm sure we all looked blank. " I hate to say this," he continued, "but I doubt whether that fellow can read or write. Do any of you have a card or paper with a lot of numbers on it?"

We each had a laissez-passer but a Mennonite conscientious objector traveling with us did not. Koop said, "Give him anything pink you have in your wallet. He gave the guard his dog's rabies vaccination certificate and we went through.

I was feeling somewhat guilty about the deception we'd foisted upon that guard until Bill said, "Literally, 'laissez passer' means 'let them pass.' I suppose if they will let us pass on a rabies vaccination card, then that counts."

Many times I have seen the Lord's provision in similar travel situations so that the work can go forward. Some years later, Bill Senn, MAP's East Africa director at the time, was traveling with a group of staff on an assessment survey. They left Nairobi early in the morning and flew to Uganda. Standing in the passport control line, Bill realized that when leaving the house he had mistakenly picked up his wife's passport instead of his own.

With the levels of unrest that fluctuate around the African continent, passport control is usually very strict. "What am I going to do now?" Bill thought. There was no way to return for his passport and continue with the scheduled itinerary.

When his turn came, Bill presented his wife's passport to the control officer, hastily explaining what had happened. The official scrutinized the passport, then looked up at Bill.

"The Bible says that when a man and woman are married, the two become one person," the officer said. Then he stamped the passport and handed it back to Bill with a smile. "Have a nice visit," he said.

From Congo we traveled to Nigeria and then to Ghana. The entire trip took us about six weeks. We visited United Presbyterian (USA) missions, Baptist General Conference, African Inland Mission, Friends, World Gospel Mission, Church of God, Church Missionary Society of England, TEAM, American Board Congregational, Methodists, American Baptists, Evangelical Free Church missions, British Baptist Disciples of Christ, Sudan Interior Mission, Sudan United Mission, Christian Reformed Church in America, Southern Baptist, and the Nazarenes. We pretty well "covered the waterfront." These contacts established many partnerships for MAP that continued for years and, along the way, enabled the Congo Protestant Relief Agency to get up and running.

As our trip came to a close, we wound up in Kenya with Jim Propst, a missionary with AIM in Kijabi. Jim was an outdoorsman and wanted us to see some real wild African animals before we left. He wasn't going to be satisfied with animals in the game park there in Nairobi. So Jim bundled us into his truck, along with all his camping gear, for an overnight trip to Amboceli. It was several hours' drive, and we had an old African gentleman who came along as a helper. To make a long story short, we never got there.

We had a flat tire along the way and had to stop and unload the truck to get the spare tire. We wound up spending the whole night trying to get to Amboceli and never got there. All we did was change tires and travel.

One memory stands out from that excursion. Chick and Gus were riding up front with Jim in the cab of the truck and I was in back with the African, huddled under a tarp trying to stay warm. Midway through the ride home, this fellow decided to take his boots off. Of course, he had no socks, and rarely had any opportunity to bathe. There's no telling how long it had been since the last time those boots came off. You can imagine the smell.

In the wee hours of Sunday morning, we finally arrived back in Nairobi. We never did see the animals, but we saw a lot of Africa that the tourists never see. That trip was a great experience for all of us. And it was a great blessing that, during the course of this trip, Chick and Gus became very close friends. That friendship lasted until Gus passed away thirty-seven years later in 1998.

Chapter Six

Adventures in the San Blas Islands

Panama, 1961

On a map you can see that the southern half of the Central American nation of Panama curves north around the Bay of Panama. If you look above the bay, to the country's Caribbean coast, you'll see "Punta San Blas," or San Blas Point. From that point, an archipelago of some eighty tiny islands curls out into the Caribbean.

The San Blas Islands are the home of the Cuna Indians, although they usually refer to themselves as the "Tule." In ancient times these Indians occupied most of the Isthmus of Panama. Cases of hereditary albinism among the Cuna gave rise to mysterious legends about the existence of white Native Americans.

I first became aware of the San Blas Indians in 1950. I had just returned to Chicago from Idaho where I had been teaching voice at Northwest Nazarene College. In my position at the Chicago Evangelistic Institute, my boss was Professor Kenneth Wells, a teacher and song-evangelist.

One day Professor Wells said to me, "I have a new student and I'd like you to teach him to sing." Of course, I agreed. The student's name was Atillio Rivera.

It soon became apparent that Atillio was not going to find success as a singer. I tried to teach him, and he tried to learn, but in the end, it was hopeless. However, during our time together, Atillio gave me a booklet about the San Blas Indians, which I read, then tucked away and forgot.

Eleven years later, in 1961, some members of the Christian Medical Society were working at the Gorgas Public Health Hospital in Panama. I kept in contact with these people and one day received a letter from them that said, "We need a plastic surgeon. If you know of anyone coming down this way, we have a two-year-old Indian boy, the son of a Cuna chief, who needs a cleft lip repair."

Sadly, as in many parts of the world, a child born deformed in the San Blas usually died at birth. The midwife would make sure that a malformed infant did not—or could not—survive.

This child had survived because he was the son of a chief. In keeping with the Cuna custom, even though the boy was two years old, he had not yet been named. Names were not given until survival was a certainty.

Providentially, I knew that Dr. Ralph Blocksma, a plastic surgeon and future MAP board member, was planning a short-term trip to Ecuador, to work with Paul Roberts, founder of the Hospital Vos Andes, a mission hospital in Quito. I told Ralph about the request I'd received from the CMS team at Gorgas Public Health Center and he agreed to stop over on his way to Ecuador to perform the boy's surgery.

In order for Ralph to stop in Panama on the way to Quito, they had to arrange a small "puddle-jumper" aircraft to land on the beach on one of the larger islands in the San Blas chain. Along with his surgical equipment, Ralph had taken an anesthesiologist from Grand Rapids. After landing, a dugout "kyooka" ferried the pair to a smaller island where Lonnie Iglesias lived.

Lonnie was a Cuna Indian whom many thought was the sole source of spiritual vigor in the San Blas Islands. Lonnie had attended Bible College in Michigan, married an American girl, and taken her back to Panama with him. At this time, Lonnie's wife, Marvel (pronounced mar-VEL) was the only foreigner living in the eighty islands. Marvel's kitchen had been selected as the site for the surgery. In addition to being the cleanest place in the islands, it also had a large kitchen table that could serve as the operating table.

Dr. Blocksma successfully repaired the cleft lip of the Cuna chief's son, and that act of mercy resulted in all the islands being opened up to the gospel. Prior to this, the fellows from Gorgas had been going over to the San Blas from Panama to do mission work, but they had always been limited to short day-trips. The Cuna observed a strong taboo that prohibited foreigners staying overnight on the islands.

Later that year, to ascertain what MAP might do to help meet the medical needs in the San Blas Islands, I made an assessment trip to the same area where Ralph had conducted his "Kitchen Clinic." When our small plane touched down on the same beach where Ralph had landed, Lonnie was there to pick me up in a *kyooku*.

As we paddled toward Lonnie's home on the island of Ailigandi, suddenly a name from the past leaped to my mind: *Atillio Rivera*. I remembered that student from the Panama islands mostly because I had failed so miserably in my efforts to teach him to sing. Up to this point, I had not thought about the possible connection between the San Blas inhabitants and my experience with a Cuna Indian at the Chicago Institute.

I asked Lonnie, "Do you happen to know anyone named Atillio Rivera?" Lonnie instantly brightened up and said, "I sure do. He's our pastor. Look up ahead and you can see him on the beach. He's waiting to see you."

When we hit the beach there were hugs and handshakes all around. It was a great thrill and surprise to encounter a former student on a remote Caribbean Island, and Atillio seemed just as happy to see me.

But then I got another, less pleasant, surprise. Atillio remembered my love for music. Now that I had come to his home, he wanted to put on a concert for me. When Atillio and his church choir gave their performance, great was my regret that I hadn't been a better teacher.

So much for my reputation in Panama as a music teacher.

Over the next few years, MAP assisted both Atillio and Lonnie's ministries, as well as the Gorgas Public Health Center, with medicines and medical supplies. It wasn't long before the Southern Baptist Mission Board built a small hospital on one of the islands and for a number of years after that, MAP provided a lot of assistance in the San Blas.

And the chief's son? He was given the name Rafael, in honor of his surgeon, Ralph Blocksma. As he grew up, the son of a chief became a "Child of the King," and today, Rafael is a pastor in Panama.

Chapter Seven

MAP and the Big Game Hunter

India and Chicago, 1962

Some people say that Robert Ruark was the greatest outdoor writer who ever lived.

A North Carolina boy born in 1915, Ruark was a reporter in Washington, D.C. before becoming a gunnery officer in the Pacific theater during World War II. After the war, Ruark became a syndicated columnist and widely read author of books on hunting, which he wrote describing his adventures on safari in Africa and India. *Horn of the Hunter* and *Something of Value* were two literary efforts which brought the writer significant fame and financial reward.

But I think Ruark's most significant contribution resulted from a column he wrote in 1962. What happened afterward is something that Ruark, himself, may never have known about.

One Monday morning in 1962, I arrived at the Christian Medical Society office in Oak Park to find that the postman had delivered two mailbags full of letters addressed to The Christian Medical Mission. The name wasn't exactly ours, but it was clearly our address on the envelopes.

None of us had any idea where such a pile of mail might have come from. Ordinarily we received a fairly small packet of mail on Monday mornings. We'd never gotten mail by the bag—and this was two bags full.

We lugged the bags up to our offices and our bookkeeper, Delores Criley, began opening the mail. Pretty soon Delores came to my office. "Ray, you'd better come look at this," she said. "We have no idea what's going on here."

There, on Delores' desk, was a substantial pile of envelopes. And every one had a check in it. But none of the envelopes contained any explanation of why the checks had been sent.

"What do we do?" Delores asked.

"Just keep opening the envelopes," I replied. "Maybe you'll find a clue about what's going on."

Sure enough, eventually one of the envelopes yielded a newspaper clipping of a column by Robert Ruark. This fellow Ruark was known as something of a renegade—certainly not the type you'd expect to have anything to do with spiritual things. Most people read his articles because of the wild adventures he encountered, and the sublime way he had of describing them. But it was a mystery to all of us what Ruark could have to do with checks being sent to our office.

The story I gleaned from that clipping was that Ruark had been tiger hunting in India. Although Ruark was quite the accomplished big game hunter, evidently the tiger got the best of him this time. Ruark was severely mauled and ended up being treated by a British missionary physician at a Swedish mission hospital—Clement Moss at Padhar Mission Hospital in Maharashtra State, northeast of Bombay (now called Mumbai).

Dr. Moss was successful in patching up the wounded outdoorsman and later, when Ruark was released, he asked about paying the bill for Dr. Moss' services.

As I recall, Ruark asked, "Dr. Moss, can't I pay you for your services?"

"No, indeed," Moss replied. "This is a Christian hospital, as you no doubt have discovered while you've been here. We don't charge for our services."

"Isn't there something I can do to help you?" Ruark asked. "Where do you get this equipment and medicine?"

Whether the name Dr. Moss gave the writer was misunderstood or became garbled in some way, we never knew. But the name "Christian Medical Mission," at the CMS address in Oak

Park was printed in the column Ruark had written, detailing the whole experience of being chewed up by a tiger, and patched up by a medical missionary.

"If you'd like to help the people who kept me alive," Ruark wrote, "this is the address. Send them some money."

At last, we knew what was happening. Letters had come in from all over the country—about two hundred of them, each with a check for five, or ten, or fifteen dollars.

This was truly a gift from God. Up until this time, CMS had resisted allowing us to raise any money from CMS members for the MAP operation. Funding was extremely tight, and we had to watch every penny simply to afford the small amount of office supplies we needed for correspondence and record keeping. These expenses had been covered primarily by service fees charged to the missions that were receiving medicines, supplies, and equipment, but that wasn't really enough to meet the needs.

Here, at last, was a source of funding that had arrived completely independent of anything that we, or CMS, had done to elicit contributions. In time, we corresponded with each of the people who had sent in a check, and a number of them continued as donors for some years. From this point in history, it's impossible to know how many of those generous people have continued to support MAP. In those days, we just didn't have the facilities to keep track of relationships with supporters all around the country. But we can look back on it now and see that this was the beginning of a significant source of support, which continues today.

From one of the most unlikely sources, a big game hunter whose pen was sharper than his aim—at least on one particular day—the Lord provided the resources to help MAP find the support to get on its feet.

Who can trace the secret workings of the unseen hand of providence? Who can say what might have happened if Ruark's aim had been better that day? It may be that had we not received that windfall of support, things could have turned out very differently. Given the funding problems, it's quite possible that at the next CMS board meeting, the directors would have said, "Ray, this program is draining time and energy, not to mention the limited funds we have. It's too bad, but we'll have to discontinue this project."

Again, who can say? But from that providential beginning, support from donors across the country continued and grew over the years, enabling a small CMS project called Medical Assistance Programs to reach out to millions of needy people around the world through a billion dollars in medical supplies distributed since MAP's beginning.

I suppose that Robert Ruark never knew the deeper impact his adventure writing had on people around the world. Ruark died in 1965 while receiving medical treatment for injuries received in another attack.

Chapter Eight

Surgical Emergencies

Honduras, 1962

In eastern Honduras, the town of Ahuas (pronounced OW-us) sits alongside the Rio Patuca, just twenty miles inland from the Caribbean coast. For missionaries in 1962, unless they were prepared to paddle a canoe upstream for twenty miles, a small aircraft was the only way in.

I was in Honduras with Dr. Gus Hemwall, a Christian Medical Society (CMS) board member and the man I considered my "mentor" in medical matters. I had traveled with Gus in Africa in 1961, and this trip was similar, as we were visiting several hospitals that were being served by CMS and MAP. A young physician, Dr.Ian Cook, and his wife staffed the hospital in Ahuas. Before taking the Ahuas assignment, Ian had just completed his internship, so Gus and I had planned a visit to encourage the young doctor and his wife.

After our Mission Aviation Fellowship (MAF) plane landed in Ahuas, we made it to the Cook's house where the young physician said to Gus, "Dr. Hemwall, I know you've performed numerous OB operations, but a lot of this is still new to me. I have a patient here with some unusual symptoms and I'm not sure of the diagnosis. Since I knew you were coming, I asked her to come back this afternoon. I'd like you to see her."

That afternoon Gus examined the girl, and I witnessed one element of missionary medical work that causes it to appeal so strongly to many physicians. Presented with a difficult case in a remote jungle clinic, lacking a lab, x-ray equipment or any other diagnostic helps, Gus had to rely on the age-old technique of diagnostic detective work done by taking the patient's history and observing her symptoms.

After the exam, Gus met with Ian and me to report, "Either she has a tumor or a problem with her ovaries. Either way, we'll have to operate."

"We can do the surgery right here, but it'll take four people" Gus said. "I'll operate. Ian's wife can serve as the scrub nurse, and since Ian knows his way around the operating room, he'll act as circulating nurse. Ray, you can be my assistant. Are you game?"

Naturally, I agreed to do whatever I could to help, and the surgery was set for early the next morning.

The Ahuas clinic really wasn't set up for surgery. Ian's wife, Linda, stayed up through the night, using a small, office-sized autoclave to sterilize all the instruments she thought we'd need.

The next morning, we made the young girl as comfortable as possible on a table and Gus administered a spinal block anesthetic. Soon, Gus had discovered that she didn't have a tumor, but she did have a problem that required immediate attention.

Gus said, "Ray, I'm going to have to do a different procedure than I was planning and it's going to take a bit longer than we thought. I'm going to have to dissect around her ovaries. If we can save them we ought to, for her sake. She's only eighteen or nineteen years old. If we can preserve her reproductive ability it will make a big difference for her in years to come. That's what I'm going to try to do." So Gus went ahead with the procedure.

About the time Gus finished and was ready to close the incision, the girl started coming to. When you administer a spinal, the medication has to be calculated in the beginning for the length of time the procedure is expected to take. It has to be right because you can't simply give more if for some reason you find that you need the patient sedated for a longer time. Since it took longer than anticipated, the anesthetic was wearing off and our patient started to moan loudly. To my shock, the moaning caused her diaphragm to press on her bowel and force it out through her incision.

Even though I was the designated "assistant," I don't think I was much help at that moment. But Gus, with the composure of one who'd operated many times under similar conditions, simply pressed the girl's bowel back in place. She moaned again, and out came her bowel again.

As I fumbled to help hold the slippery mass in its place I said "Gus, what are we going to do?"

With a glance around the room Gus said, "We need someone to calm her down while we finish, but nobody here speaks her language. I guess you could hold her bowel in while I suture around your hand. That might do it."

"You're kidding," I said.

"Yeah, I am," Gus said. "But we better think of something."

About that time, a face appeared in the tiny window of the door to our operating room. Gus called out, "Come in," and a young American woman stepped into the room. Neither of us recognized her. Gus said, "Do you speak Mosquiti?"
When the woman replied, "Yes, I do," we felt as if we had been visited by an angel. "Would you see if you could get this girl to relax long enough for us to close her up?" Gus asked.

What happened then was one of the most dramatic demonstrations I've seen of the power one person can have over another. This woman bent down near our patient and began stroking her face and hair, whispering gently in her ear in her own language. I may not have understood what was being said, but I clearly saw the effect it was having. Almost immediately I felt the girl's diaphragm relax. Gus and I pressed her bowel back into place again and quickly closed her up.

Later I learned that our "angel" was a missionary nurse, stationed at another clinic some distance away. While we were occupied with the surgery, our MAF pilot had decided to make a quick run over to this other station to make sure this young lady was getting along all right. When he arrived, the nurse had asked him to take her back to Ahuas so she could spend a few days of R&R with her friends, the Cooks. As a result, the only medical person around who could speak this girl's language walked in on our operating room emergency at exactly the right time.

That nurse may not have been an actual angel, but I felt she was definitely sent by God at that time. I don't know what we would have done if she hadn't come when she did.

A few years later, I had an opportunity to be the one who was in the right place at the right time for a different kind of operating room emergency. But things didn't turn out exactly the same way this time.

I was visiting a hospital at Nyankunde in the southeast corner of Zaire. The facility was operated as a cooperative effort by the Africa Inland Mission, the Plymouth Brethren, and the Conservative Baptist Foreign Mission Society. A good friend, Dr. Herb Atkinson, was one of the missionary physicians. Herb had to make a call on an outlying clinic at a Brethren mission in place called Lolowa, and asked me to come along.

I found myself sitting on a porch that served as the waiting room for the Africans who had come to be examined and treated by Herb. Every so often, Herb would call me in to see some particularly interesting pathology he faced; then I would return to my place on the porch.

Late in the day, I returned to the porch and there was a man—a pygmy—perched atop the low wall that surrounded the porch, sitting much like a bird might sit on a tree limb. He sat there motionless, without making a sound, for several hours, until finally, he was the last patient to be examined.

Soon after he went into the examining room, Herb called out again and said, "Ray, come in here please, I need your help."

I hurried in and asked Herb what he wanted.

Herb had the pygmy man stretched out on the examining table. He said, "I want you to lie on top of this fellow while I lance that abscess on his leg."

"What?"

"I've got to lance this fellow's abscess," Herb repeated. "I don't think it's a good idea to use any anesthetic on him, but he's going to yelp to high heaven when I open this sore. I need someone to hold him down."

I looked doubtfully at the child-sized pygmy adult and said,

"Do you know how much I weigh?"

"I've got a pretty good idea," Herb said. "That's why I called you in here."

I don't know what kind of expression that pygmy saw on my face as I stretched out over him, but when I let my full weight press him flat against the table, he must have felt as awkward as I did. He tried to throw me off, and very nearly did. I've never seen anyone who was so strong for his size.

Sure enough, when Herb lanced the abscess, that guy let out a scream and almost came off the table, even with me doing my best to hold him down.

Later, I thought back on the incident in Ahuas, and how that nurse had been able to calm the girl in surgery by stroking her face and hair and whispering in her ear. Judging from the look on that pygmy's face when I climbed on top of him, I think if I'd tried similar tactics, he might have thrown me through the roof.

I haven't had the opportunity to assist in any more operations since then, and I think it's better that the Lord should use more "angelic" nurses for those surgical emergencies.

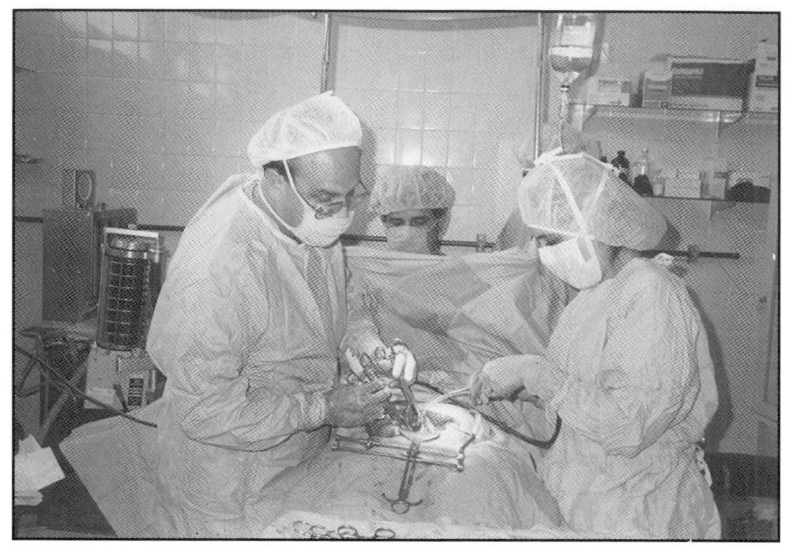

Skilled Christian doctors on short-term missions provide health and hope to a hurting world.

Chapter Nine

The Auca Hymn

Ecuador, 1963

The three men who wrote the majority of books in the Bible—Moses, David and Paul—were all murderers. Komo, an Auca Indian, was also a murderer. In 1955, when five young American missionaries were killed by headhunters on a river-bank in Ecuador, Komo had joined in the massacre.

The book about that incident and its aftermath, *Through Gates of Splendor*, inspired a generation of missionaries as it detailed the lives and deaths of those martyrs, as well as the effect that incident had on the ensuing work of missions among the Auca.

It was eight years later, 1963, and I was in Ecuador, working in Quito. Murray Weaver, a friend serving with HCJB, the missionary hospital and radio station (Heralding Christ Jesus' Blessings) mentioned that he needed to go out to a Wycliffe Bible Translators' base camp and asked me to come along.

Our "puddle jumper" aircraft landed at Limoncocha, a small town in the Shell Mera Valley, not too far from the area where those young missionaries had died. The Wycliffe ministry, called the Summer Institute of Linguistics, was doing some pioneering work in Bible translation there, and among the staff was Rachel Saint. Rachel's brother, Nate, was one of the five young men who had been killed by Komo's raiding party.

While Murray and I were in Limoncocha, I happened to meet Rachel at the little post office in town. Beth and I had known Rachel for years, so we were both happy for an opportunity to catch up on the news with each other.

"Ray, why don't you come over for tea this afternoon?" Rachel asked.

"I'd love to," I said. "Is there any special occasion?"

"We're working on translation of the New Testament into Auca," Rachel said. "I have Dayuma and her family staying at my house. They are here helping as language consultants on the project. Among these Indians, when one of them goes on a trip the whole family comes along, so they're staying in a sort of encampment behind my house.

"Dayuma was the first convert among the Auca," she explained. "And her husband, Komo, was one of the men who killed Nate and the others. Komo has also come to know the Lord. I know you'd like to meet them, and knowing your interest in music, I think you would really enjoy hearing them sing."

When I arrived at Rachel's place, a tiny, missionary-built cottage in the jungle, she said, "Ray I have a surprise I think you will really appreciate. Komo has composed the first hymn in Auca."

I was thrilled. "Is there any way you could get them to sing it for me?" I asked.

"I don't know," Rachel said. "They really are quite shy. The only way I might be able to get them to sing for you is this. They will feel very obligated if you give them something first. They will feel that they have to give you something in return. Maybe if you sing for them I could get them to sing for you."

"Well, if they can stand it, so can I," I said.

We were in the yard outside Rachel's place. She gathered the Indians around us, and I sang a few verses of "How Great Thou Art."

Shortly, Rachel was able to coax the Auca into singing in return. They launched into Komo's first effort in hymnody, the first ever written in the Auca language, and sang all twenty-two verses.

The melody went from middle C to E flat, a minor third, so the tune was quite simple. As we listened, I told Rachel that from my studies in musicology, I believed I could predict exactly the way the Auca would dance, just from the way they sang.

"Oh really?" she said.

So never having seen these Indians dance, I described to Rachel what I thought the Auca dance would be like. "You're exactly right," she said.

Rachel spoke with the ladies and then said to me, "They seem to have taken a liking to you, Ray." Turning back to the Auca women, Rachel said, "Dayuma, would you and some of the other ladies dance for Dr. Knighton?"

They agreed, rather enthusiastically. Some of the fellows ran into the forest with machetes and came running back with canes they had cut. In less time than it takes to tell it, they had whittled some simple flutes and they played while the women danced. Rachel danced with them.

It was a very simple dance, and I was gratified to see that I had described it accurately to Rachel. I had explained that the size of the range in the songs of a group like the Auca will tell you how vigorous (or non-vigorous) their dance will be. If there is not a wide range musically in the song, there will not be a wide range of vigor in the dance either. With their arms around each other's shoulders, the ladies stepped forward two or three paces, in time with the music, then back. That was it. When they were finished, it was time for the fellows to dance. Apparently, the women couldn't play the flutes, but they could sing and clap. The fellows danced to this accompaniment, and their dancing was much more vigorous as they acted out imitations of various animals in their dance.

Suddenly, one of the men stopped and with Rachel translating said, "Rachel danced with the women, so you have to dance with us!"

I gamely tried to dance along with them, and I'm sure it was a real sight, this big, lumbering guy trying to imitate a jungle animal.

Those Indians just howled with laughter. Rachel later said she had never seen those people so "cracked-up" with laughter before. In the middle of it, Rachel grabbed my camera and snapped a picture. Somewhere there is a blurry picture of me there in the jungle, dancing like an animal, with these Aucas circled around, doubled up in laughter.

I don't think that photo would make it into anyone's book of the highlights of missionary endeavor, but I like to think that they saw a different side of the missionaries that day. And I hope it made a positive impression on them. I know that my own experience of hearing that hymn, the first ever written in Auca, written and sung by some of the very people who had murdered Nate Saint, made a deep and lasting impression on me.

Chapter Ten

Hazarajat Hospital

Afghanistan, 1964

The town of Bamian sits in the mountainous central highlands of Afghanistan. On a map of the region, a line drawn from Tehran to Kabul runs almost directly through it.

The Bamian Valley is one of the few fertile spots in a dry, desert country. From the air the floor of the irrigated valley appears as a splash of green dotted with hearty trees of a deeper green and laced with dirt roads that match the color of the rugged tan mountains that rise around it.

Only about fifteen percent of the land in Afghanistan is suitable for farming and only six percent is cultivated. All of it has to be irrigated through the use of springs, streams and irrigation ditches. The white water of the old Kunduz River roars through this beautiful area within a rugged region. This is the place where the government of Afghanistan, in 1964, asked MAP to build a hospital.

It all started with a friend of ours, Christie Wilson, who had gone to Afghanistan as a teacher in a trade school. While there, he had been an encouragement to Drs. Rex and Jeanne Blumhagen, who had gone to Afghanistan as doctors with the U.S. Embassy in Kabul.

Rex and Jeanne returned to the States after a tour of duty during which Jeanne had developed quite a mastery of the

Afghan language. The couple challenged us saying, "Ray, why don't you and Beth look into the opportunities for MAP to help with the medical needs in Afghanistan?"

So it came about that I first visited Afghanistan in 1964. My contact in-country was Dr. John Hankins, a general surgeon who had trained at Johns Hopkins in Baltimore and was working in Afghanistan as a surgeon with CARE-Medico. Through his boss at CARE, John arranged an appointment for me to meet with the prime minister, Dr. Mohammad Yusof, and Dr. Zahir, his deputy prime minister, who was also a physician and a relative of King Zahir.

Until the 1960s, Afghanistan's king and his relatives had dominated the government, even though they had to work at maintaining the support of conservative ethnic and religious leaders. In 1963, for the first time, a prime minister was appointed from outside the royal family. Then, in 1964, a new constitution provided for a democratic government with a division of power between the chief executive and an elected parliament. But there was trouble from the beginning. King Zahir and the legislative branch could not agree on a reform program.

When I arrived in Afghanistan for the first time, a major power shift was in progress. Looking back on it now, I believe the circumstances may have caused Dr.Yusof to feel he needed to make some show of power. As a result, he initiated changes that might never have occurred under strict royal rule. I also believe that God was working providentially behind the scenes to position MAP in the right place at the right time.

During the meeting, as I told Dr. Yusof and his deputy about MAP and the work we were doing around the world, it occurred to me how equally providential it was that prior to this trip, MAP had been incorporated as an entity separate from the Christian Medical Society. Under the banner of our new organizational name, doors were opened for us that beforehand would have remained closed forever in countries like Afghanistan.

As we conversed about what MAP might do for them, Dr. Zahir said to me, "Isn't it interesting, Mr. Knighton, that in Afghanistan, we have never taken advantage of Christian missions like our Muslim neighbors have in Pakistan and Iran?"

I agreed, saying, "Yes, isn't it interesting, sir?" I recognized that the deputy was sending a message that required reading between the lines. He was saying that he understood who we were, and what we were about, and that he wanted us to come and help. In the years to come, Dr. Zahir would become a good friend of MAP.

We returned to the States with an agreement signed by the government, and on that basis, approached USAID for a grant for nurse midwives whom we recruited to provide medical care through mobile village clinics. Before long, Rex and Jeanne Blumhagen returned to Afghanistan as part of MAP's team.

Soon we were in possession of a protocol from the government: a preliminary draft of our agreement, planning the course of this experiment in medical outreach and outlining our code of conduct. For political reasons, the government of Afghanistan wanted to establish some medical work in the hinterlands, to show how much they cared for the people.

The approach we settled on was to provide medical care in the villages via temporary medical camps. Our equipment had arrived in Afghanistan, we had secured trucks for in-country transportation, and we had recruited short-term volunteers from various specialties. These STMs (short term missionaries) would go out for several weeks at a time under Rex and Jeanne's direction to run the clinics in areas the government would select for us.

Although the approach proved quite successful, it wasn't fully accomplishing all that the government wanted. Before long they selected a site for us to build a hospital and gave us some land in the town of Nyak, in the area of known as the Hazarajat.

Nyak definitely qualified as hinterlands. The closest place you could find on a map now would probably be the tourist town of Bamian, some forty or fifty miles from the site given to us by the government.

The entire population of Bamian had been wiped out by Genghis Khan in 1222 in reprisal for the death of his grandson, who had been killed in the siege of Bamian. Modern tourists came to see the beautiful lakes at Bandimer with their startling blue water and the colossal statues of Buddha, carved into the mountainside in the fifth and sixth centuries, one of which was one hundred seventy-five feet tall. (To the dismay of many in the international community, as this book was being written, these statues were blasted out of the mountainside by Islamic militants with rocket launchers.)

With the help of the International Afghanistan Mission (IAM), we began recruiting staff. Vincent Rutherford came aboard as construction superintendent. Vince had been a missionary with the Methodist Church, and they continued to support him. He came to Afghanistan with IAM, and then was loaned to MAP. Rex and Jeanne were on the team, as well as nurses from Britain under the Church Missionary Society, and some staff from the TEAR Fund. We started to build our hospital.

We were about halfway through the building process when King Zahir, who was passing through that part of the country, decided to stop in and see the new hospital. He was very upset that the facility wasn't being constructed to a kingly standard of elegance.

Frankly, our idea had been to build a hospital in 19th century style so it wouldn't appear too out of place for the surrounding area. But the King had other ideas. He issued a decree that halted construction while marble floors were added, together with marble that ran three quarters of the way up the walls, as well. Of course, the King paid for it all, and in the end, we had some of the most beautiful buildings in the world for our hospital, but the delay set us back nearly two years.

Once the hospital was operational we assembled a very international staff. Our radiologist was Indian; the hospital administrator was from Finland. Eventually we had a lot of Finns on the team. They loved it there because the hospital was snowed in six months of the year and it reminded them of Finland.

Being snowed in six months of each year presented a challenge that we tried to overcome by putting skis on an airplane. MAP International had, in fact, received the first permit ever issued for a private airplane license in Afghanistan. Bread for the World, in Germany, had given us a Cessna 182 for transport from Kabul up into the mountains, and Mission Aviation

Fellowship sent us a pilot and a mechanic to fly and maintain the plane for us.

The skis, intended to overcome our winter problem, created another difficulty. The weight of the skis reduced the payload so drastically that the plane couldn't take on passengers.

In time, however, we found that the snowbound status of the Nyak airstrip in the wintertime wasn't the only obstacle to air transport we would face. Once the hospital was running at full strength we began developing medical outposts in communities beyond the immediate reach of the hospital.

One of them was in a place called Panjao, southeast of Bamian. We took over a building there and set up a little hospital and clinic staffed by two nurses.

The airstrip at Panjao was on the side of the mountain and wasn't even close to being straight. It had a dogleg bend in it. If you had any kind of a crosswind, there was no way you could put the plane down. When the plane did land, local children would come running out to grab the tail of the plane and help turn it around so it could be stabilized. Then, when we took off, the kids would simply let go of the tail and the plane would fly or fall—I was never sure which—off the edge of the mountain.

On one occasion, Beth and I had the chairman of our board, Dr. Jack Hough, and his wife, Jodi, with us. We had driven a Russian jeep up the narrow dirt track that served as a road, cut into the steep slope of a very rugged mountainside. It could be quite a hair-raising trip. Some of the hairpin turns were so sharp that we had to take someone along to sit in the back with a block. When we slowed to negotiate an especially sharp turn, this fellow would hop out and put the block under the wheels to keep us from rolling back while we shifted gears. Of course there was no guardrail anywhere along that dangerous passage. It was one of those situations when you breathe a thankful sigh of relief when you simply arrive alive.

I had taken the plane on a short hop to a couple of outposts near Panjao while Beth stayed at Panjao with the Houghs. When I came back with the plane, I was to land, pick them up, and take them back to Nyak. But as we approached, there was a crosswind on the little airstrip and we couldn't risk landing.

By radio we advised Beth that we couldn't land and would have to fly back to Nyak. "You'll have to drive the jeep back down the mountain and bring the Houghs," I said.

Beth thought, "Oh, my goodness, I've got the chairman of the board, and his wife, and our nephew Doug. I'm not used to driving in mountains like these. I can't take these people's lives in my hands."

There was also an Afghan man there who needed to take his little boy down to the hospital, so they were being loaded into the jeep as well.

Beth told me, "I can't drive that road. It's just too narrow and dangerous."

So I told Beth she would have to find a driver. As it turned out, they were blessed to find an Afghan who was actually a wonderful driver and got the whole party down just as the sun was setting. As they drove up I was standing there waving and smiling, happy to see them arrive safely. Later Beth told me that when she saw me there she'd thought, "Okay, Ray. If you're so happy and relaxed, next time *you* ride down and then we'll see how you feel!"

But it wasn't only the steep mountain roads that troubled Beth in Afghanistan. She had her problems with flying as well. Whenever we flew from Kabul to the hospital we'd always have supplies and provisions to take along, as well as our personal luggage. With the cold and altitude it could be a risky flight and the pilot had to calculate the total payload exactly before he could take off. Beth said to me, "I'm not going to tell my weight to get on that plane." And she picked up some luggage and got on the scale. When the pilot asked, "How much is it?" Beth gave the combined weight of herself and the luggage. It was a beautiful flight over gorgeous country, and the pilot was very skillful, but it was always an exciting landing.

Marta Brunner, a German nurse, and Pat Cook, a nurse from England, were in charge of the clinic at Panjao. One evening they asked Beth and me to stay the night. I found out later that they were treating the first rabies patient they'd had there. They were trying desperately to keep alive a brave man who had been bitten by a rabid wolf.

The Afghans had told us that a rabid wolf would proceed on a straight line along whatever course its diseased brain was directing it. If anyone were in its way, the animal would attack and this wolf had killed a number of people as a result. The man Pat and Marta were treating had actually rammed his arm down the wolf's throat to kill it. But now, he lay dying. No one there had ever been known to survive rabies. What confidence it would inspire in the local people if our staff could take a hero like that, known to be infected with rabies, and pull him through.

So Marta and Pat worked through the night, following a textbook that told them what to do for a rabies patient. I stayed up helping them, but by morning the man had expired. Marta and Pat were just heartbroken. They had worked so hard trying to save that man's life.

Later I had occasion to ask Pat, "With the problem of wolves as it is here, how do you survive when you go out to deliver babies on house calls?"

Pat said, "I take an Afghan with me and he carries a lamp and a musket. But the other night I went out to deliver a baby and on the way back we were surrounded by a pack of wolves. The Afghan got scared as the wolves were circling and closing in."

"What did you do?" I asked.

"Simple," she said. "I just started singing. My singing is so bad that no one can stand to be near me. But I have to admit I was a little surprised to find that even wolves will keep their distance."

The wolves were probably the only ones who kept their distance from MAP's medical workers in Afghanistan. The community embraced the hospital from the first day. People still refer to that building as MAP's building. It got to the point that people would bypass the university hospital in Kabul and travel up to the MAP hospital high in the mountains for treatment. Not only did we have medicines, but we served with a compassionate care that often could not be found anywhere else in the country. In 1964, political changes had opened the door for MAP International in Afghanistan. In 1973, political changes were closing that door. During 1973 I made four trips to Afghanistan, trying to keep the door open. The government officials wouldn't talk to anyone locally so I would have to go there and meet with the officials. They would renew our permission to stay, but in three months they'd be ready to throw us out, and I'd have to go back and secure the hospital's status again. As Christians, we had become a political liability for a new government that was turning sharply in another direction. We tried to instruct our staff to keep a low profile as Christian believers. But it's very difficult for a believer working with sick and needy people to keep quiet about the highest motivation in his or her life.

By the summer of 1973 the government was making demands that finally forced us to leave. On Thursday, July 12, I met with the minister of health, Dr. Kosbeen. It wasn't long before I knew that our proposal for a year to continue with the hospital while we tried to work out a new agreement was not going to be accepted.

They wanted us to continue providing medicines, supplies, equipment, and people, while they sent in Afghan doctors and administrators to take over the hospital and the nursing centers and run them as government facilities. We couldn't comply.

Dr. Kosbeen said, "In a few days, when you receive a letter, your current protocol will be canceled."

I guess I was expecting that. But then Dr. Kosbeen said something that surprised me greatly. He said that one of the reasons they were doing this was that the Christian hospital, as he called it—Nyak—was doing such excellent work that it was showing up the government hospitals so badly that they couldn't stand the competition.

We talked for some time after that, but it was already clear to me that MAP was finished in Afghanistan. My report for that day, which we have on file in MAP's archives, includes this observation: "Apparently, there's a great struggle going on in the government, and a lot of us are getting the backlash from it."

Less that a week later, on July 18, 1973, Prince Daoud, the cousin and brother-in-law of King Zahir, announced on nationwide radio that the monarchy had come to an end. The democratic Constitution of 1964 was annulled, and a temporary government and a revolutionary council—both headed by Daoud—came into power.

For nearly a decade, from 1964 to 1973, MAP had conducted what I believe was a truly exceptional medical mission in Afghanistan. From 1968 to 1973, we had operated the only hospital that has ever borne the name of "MAP International." It was an exciting time in our lives and in the life of MAP. I suppose that only in eternity will we learn the full extent of the results that were achieved for the people we served, both spiritually and physically.

Arnie Newman, Web Carrol and Ray Knighton, depart Wilson airport in Nairobi, Kenya, for missions trip to Uganda, 1978.

MAP's staff say their goodbyes while waiting for relief shipment to leave for Honduras. Left to right are: Vic and C.G. Rosser, John Garvin, Phil Craven, Bill Walker (pilot) and his wife Ida, Ray and Beth Knighton, and Paul Thompson, former MAP president. Ca. 1998.

Several members of MAP's board of directors, and office staff pose outside MAP's Wheaton, Illinois, offices, ca. 1985.

Larry Dixon, former MAP president and Dr. Richard Fix inspect MAP's distribution center in Brunswick, GA.

Ray and Beth Knighton on their wedding day, October 15, 1943.

Ray Knighton, Rev. George Hoffman, director of Tear Fund, and Peter Renee inspect local handicrafts in Bangladesh, early 1970s.

Eugene Kinney, president of Zenith Hearing Aid, receives ceremonial spears in gratitude for funding of African relief, 1969.

Leo Brown, general manager of the American Medical Association, and Jack DeZault, executive director of the World Medical Association, present plaque to Ray Knighton, ca. 1970.

Ray Knighton and Larry Dixon, former president of MAP, inspect a pallet of medicines and medical supplies in MAP's distribution center, Wheaton, Illinois, ca. 1970.

John Stucky, former MAP vice-president, and David Knighton (seated) meet at MAP display during Urbana Missionary conference, Urbana, Illinois, 1971.

Ken. Gieser, M.D. (founder of the Christian Medical Society) and Beth Knighton survey construction of MAP's headquarters in Carol Stream, Illinois. Ca. 1978.

Santo Domingo clinic in the Dominican Republic, receives MAP's medicines, 1973.

Ray Knighton poses with the staff of Mattru Hospital in Sierra Leone.

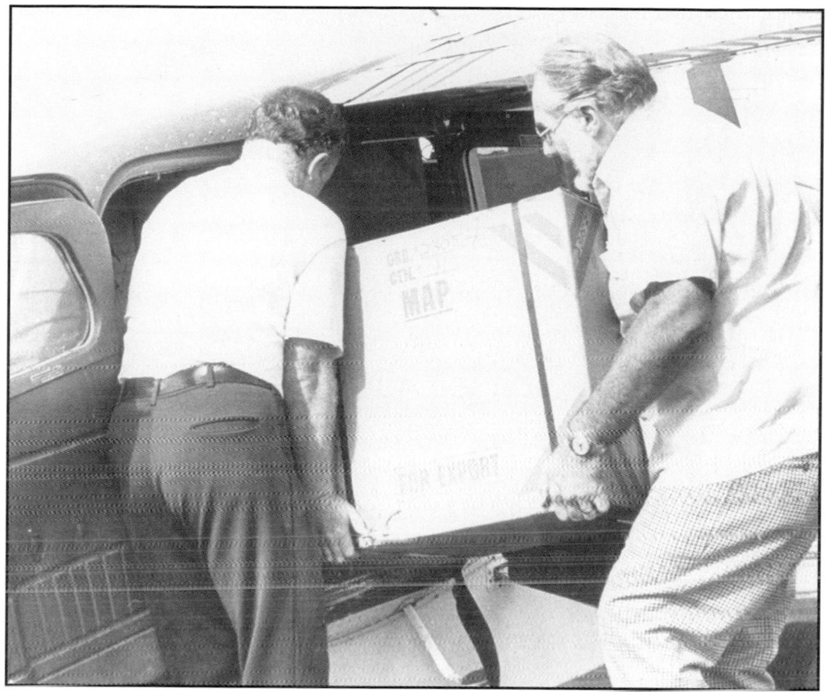

Ray Knighton and friend load medical supplies for Uganda relief, 1978.

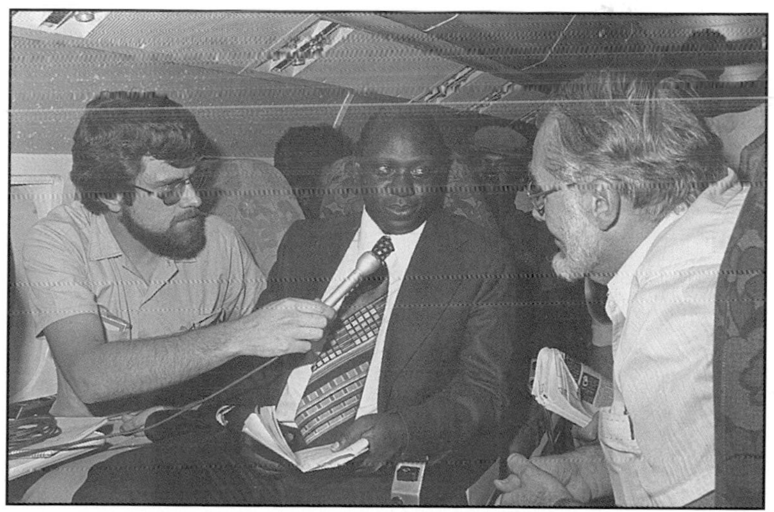

Dick Sensig, MAP public relations, and Ray Knighton meet with Uganda's provisional leader (successor to Idi Amin) on flight for Ugandan relief, 1979.

At an airport in Uganda, Ray Knighton off-loads a plane containing AIM (African Inland Mission) medical relief, 1979.

Pallets of medicines and medical supplies for Uganda relief are delivered in 1979.

HEED/Interserve (Health Education & Economic Development) mission team discusses medical shipment for Dacca, Bangladesh in early 1970. Seated from left to right are the Reverend George Hoffman of the Tear Fund, Ray Knighton, and Ray Windson.

A C130 military cargo plane is being loaded for shipment of medicines to Dacca, Bangladesh, early 1970.

Bill Pollard (attorney), Norm Finke (auditor), Howard Koop (contractor), and Beth Knighton, pose on a tractor at ground breaking for MAP's headquarters in Carol Stream, Illinois, 1978.

Ray Knighton addresses an ICMM (International Conference on Medical Missions) assembly, Wheaton, Illinois, 1970.

Ray Knighton, and Malcolm Forsberg, SIM (Sudan Inland Mission) missionary, inspect MAP medicines, ca. 1972.

In MAP's distribution center in Carol Stream, Illinois, staff is preparing a medical shipment destined for Uganda, late 1960s.

Beth Knighton purchases a "mola" weaving from craftsman in Alighandi, San Blas.

Ray Knighton points to one of the developing countries receiving assistance from MAP International, 1974.

Ray Knighton addresses conferees at Monrovia, Liberia, conference, 1972.

Ray Knighton takes care of business from his office at MAP's headquarters in Carol Stream, Illinois, 1974.

Ray Knighton boldly crosses a bamboo bridge in Bangladesh, 1971.

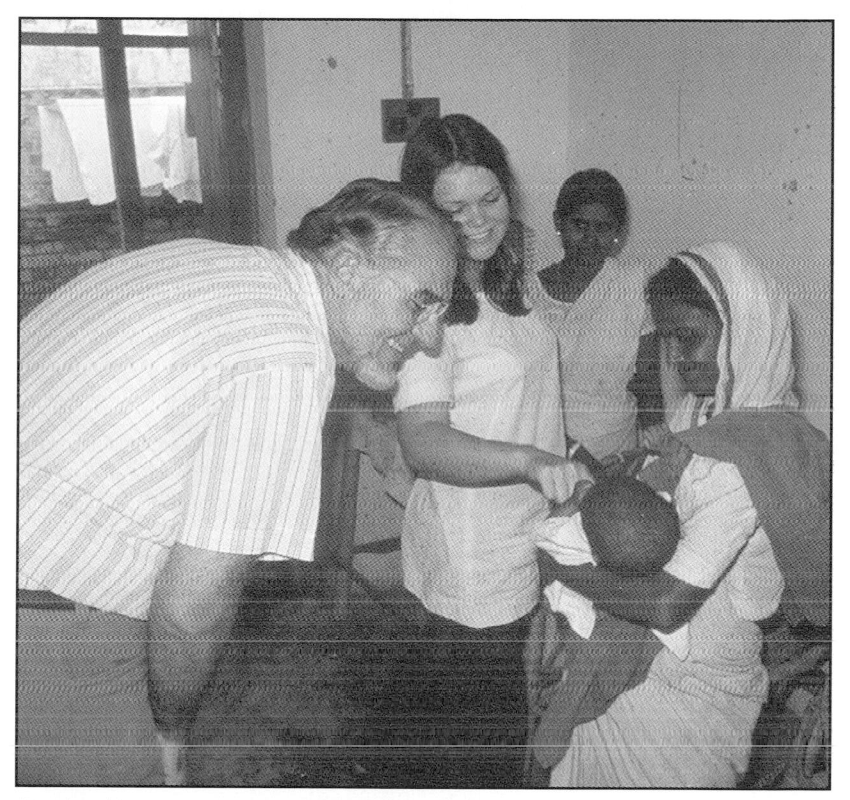

During his 1971 trip to Bangladesh, Ray Knighton is greeted by a missionary nurse who was attending a newborn baby.

Ray Knighton, Everett Van Reken, Bob Weidemeir, and Howard Moffett from Taegu Presbyterian Hospital in South Korea, break ground for MAP's headquarters in Carol Stream, Illinois, 1978.

Ray Knighton, Howard Kresge (State Dept.), Gerald Ford (speaker of the house and future U.S. president), and Ralph Blocksma meet in Ford's office to secure freight funding.

MAP's staff reviews an artist's rendering of Carol Stream, Illinois, headquarters. Ray's secretary, Amy Anderson (wearing glasses), stands at the top left-hand corner of the rendering. 1978.

Chapter Eleven

Walking with Angels

Peshawar, Pakistan, 1965

From my point of view, everything was going wrong on this trip.

It was raining in the dry season. The rain had cancelled my flight, which meant I'd have to travel by train, alone at night, through dangerous and unfamiliar territory, in a country where I didn't speak the language. Phone calls to the missionary doctor I was going to see had not gone through. I was very anxious.

Looking back on it now, I realize a lot of people in the Bible had the same sort of experience right before they saw angels.

In the Old Testament, Jacob was alone and destitute, fleeing for his life through the night when he encountered an angel of the Lord. In the New Testament, Joseph was anxious and fretful, engaged to a girl carrying a child he knew he hadn't fathered, when the angel of the Lord came to him. Later on, far from home, with nowhere to stay and Herod's killers searching for the newborn boy, the angel appeared to Joseph again.

Perhaps I should have known that I was in good company.

It was a Friday and I was coming out of Afghanistan after working with out team for a couple of weeks. I was on my way to Pakistan, for a meeting with a group of missionary physicians.

The trip had already been difficult. Unexpected dry-season downpours had crippled air traffic out of Kabul. I had to take a taxi down the Khyber Pass to Peshawar, hoping to catch a plane to Rawalpindi. From there I could get a taxi.

To my disappointment the flight out of Peshawar had also been canceled but I felt I couldn't disappoint the physicians coming for the meeting. Dr. Barkley suggested the midnight train to Karachi, which would pass through Taxila.

I wasn't keen on the idea of traveling alone by rail, but we went ahead and bought a ticket on the train scheduled to leave at five that afternoon. My apprehension about the train was only increased when it arrived late. I said a prayer, bargaining with the Lord. If the train didn't arrive in time to leave by seven, I would take it as confirmation that rail travel was unsafe. I wasn't thrilled when the train chugged into the station at 6:55 that evening.

This train was like many seen operating all over India. There was no center aisle running the length of the car so there was no conductor working the aisle. The compartment doors opened directly to the outside, and the conductor worked on the platform at the stops.

I got into my compartment and found that a Pakistani man was traveling with me. I was happy to find that he spoke English, and even more thrilled when he said he knew the railways and would be happy to let me know when we got to Taxila.

I was thinking that at last, everything would be fine, and my apprehension was just starting to subside, when my Pakistani companion climbed up into the upper bunk and promptly fell asleep. Within minutes he was snoring heavily. In our brief conversation I had learned he was going all the way to Karachi—another two days past the Taxila stop! I had no idea how long he would sleep, but from the sound of it he was planning to hibernate.

I sat fretting as the train clattered along the tracks toward Karachi, wondering how I would know when we got to Taxila. When we crossed a river I knew we were at Campbelspur and thought the next stop would be Taxila.

While I sat there stewing, I came up with a plan. I would trick some other passengers into letting me know when we arrived at Taxila. When the train creaked to a stop in the next town I threw the door open, leaned out over the platform, and shouted in what I hoped would sound like the voice of a railroad conductor, "TAXILA!"

I waited. When no one appeared out of the cars on either side of me I figured that either we were not there yet, or else everyone was hibernating like my Pakistani friend.

At the next stop I did my conductor routine again. This time I was rewarded to see several passengers clamber out the cars up and down the line. I figured we had arrived.

It was one a.m. and pitch dark on the lonely platform. By the time I had scrambled out of the car with my suitcase, my briefcase with recorder, notes and everything else, I was the only one there. A single, desolate light bulb at the far end of the planking seemed to be losing its struggle with the darkness around it.

I saw another faint light flickering inside a shanty so I crossed a rickety walkway toward the station where I found an old gentleman sorting mail. When I said, "Taxila?" he nodded "Yes." Emboldened by this success at communicating with the locals I said "Tonga?" referring to a horse-drawn taxi. This time he shook his head "No."

I probably looked a forlorn figure, standing there alone in the dark amid streaks of spattering rain illuminated by the dim glow from that single bulb.

I looked up to see three ominous figures coming toward me—turbaned silhouettes with robes flowing in the darkness. They moved noiselessly into the edge of the light. They were hard-looking Pakistani men with heavily bearded, dark faces concealed in shadow.

I don't know whether I sounded frightened or stupid, but I managed to stammer three phrases. "Taxila. Christian Hospital. Christy."

To my surprise, one of the shadows spoke—in English.

"Yes, I know Dr. Christy," he said. It was very good English.

"I'm supposed to be at that hospital," I said.

"Fine," the shadow replied. "I'll take you."

Immediately he reached for my briefcase. I wouldn't let it go. He tried my suitcase. I held on to that too, but he twisted it out of my hand and gave it to one of the others who slapped it atop his head. All three started off down the road.

In the rain the road felt greasy with mud underfoot. It was nearly impossible to keep up but as I slipped along behind them the spokesman gave me the story that they had been to a volleyball tournament out of town and were on their way to work at a cement factory next to the hospital. It sounded fishy to me. Every step I took I just knew I was going to end up with a dagger in my back.

Suddenly, an old rattletrap of a bus came rumbling out of the dark and slid to a stop. That bus was at least thirty years old and looked like it wouldn't last another thirty seconds. But we all got on and within a few minutes I saw up ahead a big, beautiful sign, glowing like a beacon in the night. In English lettering the sign said: "Christian Hospital."

"This is where I want to be," I yelped. But my guide was already ahead of me and moving to get off. I fumbled in a pocket for some rupees but he said, "No. I'll go in with you."

It was a good thing. The chokedar (guard) at the hospital gate was a tough-looking Pushtu holding a double-barrel musket and a leash with a hungry guard dog straining at the other end. Even with my turbaned attendant to speak his language, I don't think the chokedar was happy about letting us through the gate.

Inside, we found ourselves standing in the middle of a compound. On one side we could see the hospital's main building. On the other side were several houses. The guard left to find Dr. Christy.

As we waited, I reached into my jacket, thinking I'd give the fellow a few rupees for his trouble. He wouldn't have it. When he saw what I was doing held up his hands and said, "No, you just tell God what a good friend I've been."

Then, I heard some noise and turned to see Dr. Norville Christy bustling toward us, sputtering in anger.

"Ray! What are you doing here at this time of night? You know better than to do this kind of thing!" Clearly I had done something very wrong.

Thinking that my turbaned companion could reassure Dr. Christy, I turned to introduce him and found that he was gone. My gaze quickly scanned the compound, but there was no sign of the dark man in the flowing robe.

Oblivious to my confusion, Norville was busy blistering my ears.

"I'd never walk down that road by myself at night," he said. "Never. This is the most dangerous country in the world. It's a wonder you got here alive."

So I told him the story of my journey from Peshawar.

"That's impossible," Norville blurted. "I'm the physician for this cement factory and I can tell you there isn't a man here who speaks English that well. And there certainly isn't anyone there who would have taken care of you like that!"

We stood there for a moment while I tried to think of a reply but all I could say was, "Well, here I am."

Later that summer I was up at Wheaton's Honey Rock Camp in a Bible study with Dr. V. Raymond Edman. He related a story to me that he has told in his book *Wiser Than They Thought*, of a time in Ecuador when a mysterious stranger had delivered him from a very dangerous situation. When I recounted my experience on the midnight train to Karachi, he wasn't at all surprised.

"Ray that was a guardian angel!" he said. "They don't go around in white robes, you know. They're always dressed like the people around them. Thank God for His providence. You were blessed to have an angel like that accompanying you."

I believe Dr. Edman was right, and now I can look back over many years and see God's blessing and providence at work in countless ways.

One of the greatest blessings for Beth and me has been the joy of seeing God at work in so many different circumstances in our lives, and in the lives of the people we've met. It's been a blessing to know so many godly nationals. We are blessed with precious friends in countries all around the world, and we pray for them every day. It's been a tremendous blessing to have spent time with so many people that some would call "saints."

And today, it's a blessing now to be spending time at MAP's offices each week, encouraging those who are carrying the ministry forward. It's a joy to share with them the incredible story of what God has done through the work of MAP International.

Chapter Twelve

It's a Small World

Chicago and Bangladesh, 1965 and 1977

It's amazing how often a friendship developed through MAP has played an important role in our lives later on.

Over the years, many missionary doctors passing through the Chicago and Wheaton areas dropped in for a visit at the MAP offices. One day in 1965, Bethel Fleming paid a visit to our warehouse in the Stewards Foundation building on Wacker Drive in Chicago.

Bethel, and her husband Robert, were two of the first missionaries in Nepal. Robert was a world-class ornithologist, and the Nepalese government had contracted him to do some work relating to various species of birds in Nepal. Bethel, being Robert's wife and a medical doctor, was able to start the first hospital for the United Missions in Nepal.

Bethel was in the States on furlough when she came to visit our warehouse. Ever since we began to receive medical donations we had been looking for some office space with a warehouse connected to it. We were thrilled to finally find space in the Stewards Foundation building. There was an unused floor in the building we were able to rent for use as our first real warehouse, as well as a freight elevator, enabling us to move the medicines up and down.

I vividly remember walking Bethel through our warehouse that day. Although it was nothing like the size of the distribution center at our Georgia headquarters, Bethel was overwhelmed.

"I've never seen such a thing as this before," she said. "How much of these supplies could I have?"

"Bethel," I said. "If you can use them, you can have them all." She just stood there for a moment, and then started to cry. It was the beginning of a long-term relationship. Over the years, Bethel's Shanta Bawan Hospital in Katmandu received many shipments of medicines and supplies from MAP's warehouse.

At the time of Bethel's visit, our son Mike was just 8 years old, but by 1977 he was a college-age young man with some grown up ideas, who wanted to see the world and gain some grown up experience. So Mike went to Bangladesh as a short-term volunteer, working with MAP's program in Kamalganj to help build a leprosy hospital. At Wheaton College's Honey Rock Camp, Mike had learned to do electrical work, so he was assigned to all the hospital's ceiling fans and wiring.

Mike is a gregarious person and he relished participating in the lives of the people in Bangladesh, so it was natural that he found himself attending a Bengali wedding. And it was just as natural that Mike would eagerly partake of all the refreshments provided for the wedding guests—including some locally prepared—which resulted in a very severe attack of gastroenteritis.

It happened that Beth and I were making a routine visit to the MAP work at Kamalganj at that very time, and I thank God that we were present.

Mike became so ill with vomiting and diarrhea during the night that there was genuine fear that he would not make it to morning. Dr. Diane Smith's demeanor was grim as she relayed a veiled prognosis that would strike fear into any parent's heart. "Michael is gravely ill," she said.

All night long I stayed by Mike's side, helping him to the toilet, then holding him up while the sickness convulsed his body. The toilets in that part of the world, even today, are often little more than a hole in the floor with spaces for your feet on either side. Mike was getting so weak, I had to stand and hold him up.

And there were no lights. The generator that provided electricity for the hospital was turned off at 10 p.m. each night. A couple of flashlights and a candle burning in the room emitted all the light we had.

All through the night, between Mike's seizures, Beth and I prayed desperately that Mike would pull through. That night, Beth and I learned heartfelt sympathy for the countless parents throughout the developing world. Many keep watch through the night by the sides of suffering children, not knowing whether they would be alive at daybreak. That night, we gained a deeper understanding of the power and the comfort of the grace of God, who really is able to turn darkness into light.

Mike was better the next morning. With pressing business forcing Beth and me on to the next leg of our journey, we were thrilled to be able to leave Mike in the care of a Canadian physician and his wife, Don and Marylou Clunas.

Mike's recovery from this episode took so long that the doctor and his wife took him into their home and kept him for three months. While he was there, the doctor taught Mike the Bengali language, so that when he was fully recuperated, Mike was able to supervise the electrical workers in their own language. The experience stayed with Mike to such a degree that even today he sometimes breaks into the Bengali language, seemingly without thinking.

Some months later Mike and his roommate, a British fellow also working on the leprosy hospital, visited Nepal, planning to see how far they could climb on Mt. Everest. The boys made it as far as the first base camp, at 18,000 feet, when both of them became deathly ill. To this day we don't know whether it was altitude sickness or something they ate. The guide became frightened because Mike and his friend were so sick. Evidently fearing that he would be held responsible, he abandoned the boys on the mountain to come down alone.

After the experience of Mike's sickness in Bangladesh, and knowing the risk of the climb they planned, we gave Mike specific instructions: "If anything happens to you, head for the Shanta Bawan hospital."

Mike told us later that he virtually crawled into Shanta Bawan, so sick he could barely stand, and too weak to say much more than, "I'm Ray Knighton's son. Please help me!"

And they did.

By this time Bethel Fleming, and her husband Robert, had retired and returned to the States. But the relationship with Bethel's hospital, started in the warehouse in the Stewards Foundation building, and continued through the years with shipments of medicines and supplies from MAP, was still warm and fresh.

Mike and his friend were tucked into beds, rehydrated, and soon back on their feet, returning to their work at the leprosy hospital.

Yes, we know that the good people at Shanta Bawan would have taken care of Mike, even if they had never heard of Ray Knighton. But it gave us a special feeling of warmth and refreshment to know that in the mountains of Nepal, on the far side of the world from our office in Chicago, there was a hospital run by friends who would eagerly take care of our adventurous son, Mike.

People often say, "It's a small world." But I think it only seems that way because God is so big.

Chapter Thirteen

A New Beginning

Oak Park, Illinois, 1965

The power of God is so vast, and the scope of His providence so broad, that ultimately, he is able to cause even the anger and impatience of men to praise him. I think this is what Psalm 76:10 means when it says, "Surely the wrath of men shall praise thee . . ." God is able to cause "all things to work together for good," as Romans 8:28 promises, and "all things" must include the wrath of men.

By the summer of 1965, I could see that I wasn't going to be able to continue managing both CMS and MAP. MAP was becoming so well known, and so much needed, that I simply couldn't manage the demands of both organizations.

The fact was that MAP was taking up a lot of my time and a considerable amount of the money of CMS, and there wasn't enough to go around in the first place. I have no doubt that if the question had been put to the CMS board in this way: "I can't continue to manage both. Either MAP or CMS has to go. Which will it be?" The board would have voted to let MAP drop out of existence.

It quickly became clear that this was going to be an important issue at the November board meeting in Oak Park and I had written out my resignation in advance. In fact, the discussion did become quite heated and Dr. Ralph Blocksma, chair of the board at that time, was forced to resolve the argument by reading my resignation from the directorship of CMS.

After my resignation was read, he, Ken Gieser, Gus Hemwall, Everett VanReken, Bob Wilkrick, and I went to a restaurant across the street and into a meeting I would later recognize as the first board meeting of MAP International.

"Why don't we incorporate Medical Assistance Programs of CMS as a separate entity and take that on as our ministry?" I suggested.

Of course, I realized later that we had been moving toward an arrangement like this in our planning for the Africa trip with Koop and Hemwall. The name "Christian Medical Society" had built-in connotations in certain parts of the world, where "Medical Assistance Programs" would have a more neutral reception.

Our group had always seen CMS as a spiritual ministry operating in a realm of physical need, and they thought MAP could also be a ministry with spiritual impact through physical service.

In the end, we agreed that there was probably room for both organizations, and MAP could provide the basis for a ministry with which all of us could be involved.

One member of our group went back to the hotel and gave this as our report and the remaining CMS board members voted in agreement.

CMS gave us the names of three thousand inactive donors, twenty-five hundred dollars, and a few pieces of old office furniture. More important in the long run, Amy Anderson, Al Varner, and Henry Harvey also joined me in the new venture.

This was on a Friday. On Saturday I went into the office and cleaned out my desk and on Monday morning we found another office space. We opened up the first office of MAP in a rented space above a drug store on Main Street in Glen Ellyn.

If funds had been tight as part of CMS, the financial purse strings were even tighter with MAP as a separate organization. Beth had come aboard as our office manager, which was her first job with MAP. On several occasions, as payday was approaching, Beth would come to the office and say, "Ray, tomorrow is payday and there's not enough money to pay the employees."

We would all pray together about the need and invariably by the next morning we'd receive a check from some unexpected source, usually just enough to pay the employees and perhaps settle a few bills or buy some office supplies. That literally happened over and over again. Even after we had brought in more people and the expansion of MAP was underway, we always had the money to pay the employees.

God always answered a lot of prayers. One time Beth was asked, "What did you do in the office when you couldn't find things?" A lot had been dumped in our laps—a lot of responsibility to handle and very little space and personnel. Our approach to missing necessities was very simple—we'd look as hard as we were able, then if we couldn't find it, we'd pray Soon, the Lord would give one of us an impression as to where to look, and we'd always find what we were looking for.

Eventually Dr. Walter Spitzer, a young physician from Canada, became executive director of CMS and then subsequently became a MAP board member. Good relations with CMS have continued since that time with CMS recruiting students for MAP's Reader's Digest International Fellowship (RDIF) program and MAP providing medicines and supplies for their medical group missions

Children of Africa.

Chapter Fourteen

Thanksgiving in Congo

Congo, 1967

It was Thanksgiving Day, 1967. I didn't know it at the time, but the Lord was preparing to teach me a lesson about thankfulness—a lesson I would always remember.

I was in Kinshasa, the capital of Congo, which later was renamed Zaire, and more recently renamed the Democratic Republic of Congo. I was on my way to see Dr. Carl Becker, a physician at the mission hospital at Nyankunde. The nearest place with an airport was the town of Bunia, just south of the equator in central Africa, so that's where I was headed on a warm November 25th.

At 6 a.m. the airport in Kinshasa was already packed with a density of people I wouldn't have thought possible if I hadn't been there. The place was just bedlam. Many of the travelers had animals with them, along with huge bundles of stuff they were transporting across the country. I don't speak a word of French, so I thought, "How in the world am I going to get where I need to go? I can't read the signs. I can't talk to anyone." So I talked to the Lord.

At the end of my prayer I said, "OK, Lord. I'm going to do something which may be bold and may be foolish, but I don't know what else to do. I know I've done many foolish things, but You have always taken care of me. I'm trusting You to take care of me now."

I had noticed a young boy, maybe fourteen or fifteen years old, who seemed to be working as a sort of "go-fer" behind the counter. I got his attention and motioned to him to come over. He squirmed through the crushing thickness of humanity and made his way to me. Up close, the lad looked eager and bright, and although we had no language in common, I felt we could reach a common understanding.

I showed him my ticket, then handed him some money, my passport, and my ticket. I knew full well that I had just put my life in this boy's hands, without knowing whether I'd ever see any of those vital items again. But I felt I had no other alternative. I'd looked for an adult I felt I could trust and had found no one. Thankfully, half and hour later, the boy reemerged, from the throng, took me by the hand and led me through the crowd back to the departure area.

The boy put me on a plane that I thought was headed for Bunia, but I soon learned that our destination was Kisangani, Congo's second largest city. As we flew northeast over the heart of the Congo, I met a Lebanese businessman who spoke English. I didn't know it at the time, but I was soon going to need this man's assistance.

At the airport in Kisangani, I presented my papers at the ticket counter and was shocked to hear the attendant say, "This ticket is no good. You didn't pay for it in local currency. You cannot get on the plane with this ticket."

"But I've got to get to Bunia," I pleaded. Just then, the businessman I'd met on the plane approached, and I said, "Can you help me out?"

After a quick discussion, he offered to take American money in exchange for the Congolese funds I needed for the ticket. He figured out an exchange rate and I was able to buy my ticket.

But then, when I got out to the plane, the ticket-taker said, "This is Thursday. There is no plane to Bunia until Saturday."

"Well, they sold me a ticket for this plane," I said. "And I'm going on this plane." I went and found my suitcase, hauled it over, and put it on the plane myself.

That started a very animated discussion among the flight crew and airport workers. One would come over to me and say, "Okay, you're on this plane." Then another would come up and say, "No, you cannot go on this plane. This plane isn't going to Bunia."

Eventually the plane took off with me on it, but all I could do was hope that it was headed in the right direction.

The next time we touched down we were in a place called Opala, southwest of Kisangani. The crew informed the passengers that we all had to get off and go through a customs control check. As I rose from my seat to leave the plane I was shoved back into my seat. It quickly became clear that there was a Congolese man on board who was supposed to exit the plane first. Apparently, this man was a local dignitary of some sort. As his foot hit the stairs leading down from the plane, a little rag-tag band struck up a tune and paraded around below the aircraft as he got off.

Finally they let the rest of us off, and I made my way over to a little thatched hut where I was directed to get my papers checked. In the hut sat a woman nursing a baby. I put my ticket and passport on the counter and waited. After a while she recognized that I was there, got up, did something indeci pherable to my papers, then motioned that I was free to go. I returned to the plane, which soon was airborne again, this time making its way toward the southwest. A few hours later, we landed in Bunia.

During the day's adventure, zigzagging across the Congo, there had been no way to call ahead, and there was no phone in the Bunia airport. There I sat, waiting, until evening began to fall and it became apparent that the airport was closing.

The flight crew from the Air Congolese plane passed by as they were leaving and offered me a lift. "We can give you a ride into town in our pickup truck," they said. "There's no sense staying out here. The airport is closing soon, and there are no taxis."

Just then, a car pulled up outside. It a missionary I knew from Bunia— Pete Brashler, the field director for Africa Inland Mission.

"How did you know I was coming?" I asked.

"We didn't," Pete said. "But when I heard the plane coming over I thought I'd better come and check. Usually, there are no flights in here on Thursday."

Together we rode back to Nyankunde. It turned out that they were having a big Thanksgiving dinner that night with all the American missionaries in Bunia. I believe I was more thankful for that dinner than any other I can remember.

Chapter Fifteen

A Home of Our Own

Wheaton, Illinois, 1968

One day in 1968, I was having lunch with one of our board members, Dr. Kenneth Gieser, head of the Wheaton Eye Clinic. During lunch, I mentioned that I had to leave soon to drive to Dundee. Not realizing that I made the trip almost every day, Ken asked what business I had in Dundee.

"Somebody's got to be responsible for our warehouse out there," I said. "We've got a young fellow named Larry Dixon overseeing it, but ultimately I'm responsible. I make regular trips out there to make sure things are running smoothly."

"Doesn't that take a lot of time?" Ken asked.

"It sure does," I said. "I spend a lot of time on the highway. It's a twenty-five mile trip one way."

"Why don't we have a warehouse here in Wheaton?" Ken asked.

"There is nowhere in this area where we can rent a warehouse," I replied.

"Then why don't we build our own?" Ken said.

"I can think of two reasons," I said. "We don't have any land, and we don't have any money. Other than that, I suppose there's nothing stopping us."

Rather than acknowledge my facetiousness Ken simply said, "We ought to think about starting a building fund."

A few days later Ken called me at the office.

When we subdivided the Gundersen Drive development Wheaton, Carl Gundersen, Bob VanKampen, and I were principal investors. Each of us received certain parcels of land as part of our compensation. I've got an acre out there and there's an acre next to it I think we can secure."

The next thing I knew, MAP ended up with a three-acre parcel of land donated by Ken and Kay Gieser. With the land secured, half of the objection I had raised was removed. We started planning for a new building.

It also happened that Ken was a good friend of an architect in Wheaton. Soon after we received the land, this fellow came to see me. We began brainstorming plans for the office and warehouse space MAP needed. As he started drawing up plans for us to think about, we brought Larry into the discussion. As a young man growing up on a farm, Larry had gained some experience in construction, and his knowledge was a big help. He fit perfectly in the role of construction supervisor as we decided on a building plan and moved ahead with construction.

Then we ran into another obstacle that we hadn't anticipated. We couldn't find a contractor who would work with us because we didn't have anything to put up as security.

Just when it looked like that obstacle might bring the whole thing to a halt, Bill Pollard, MAP's attorney at the time, introduced us to some people he knew at KPK Construction Company. One of the principals in KPK had been a classmate of Bill's in law school. Bill's recommendation was enough security for this fellow, so KPK came on as our general contractor.

Eventually the building was financed through a Christian bank in Evergreen Park, Illinois, and the construction proceeded uneventfully. We were blessed to be able to come up with the funds needed. In addition to contributions from board members, a number of mission boards put up some money, and we received some grants from the Kresge Foundation.

When we finally took occupancy of that building, it was just wonderful to have our own space. We had purposely overbuilt so even though by that time MAP was employing nearly one-hundred people, we were able to rent out some of the extra space. Later, we added a second story for our offices.

It was also great to be part of the Christian community of organizations that also settled along Gundersen Drive. Tyndale House Publishers, famous for the *Living Bible*, was located right across the street. *Christianity Today*, which became one of the leading journals of evangelical Christianity, was just down the street. The National Association of Evangelicals, World Relief, Youth for Christ, The Evangelical Alliance Mission (TEAM), Christian Service Brigade and others were all located nearby.

The development consortium had donated, or sold reasonably, the land for all these organizations.

When we finally left Wheaton, a group of orthopedic surgeons approached us with an offer to buy the building. Each of these physicians had been partners with MAP in various efforts, so in a sense, we felt that the building was staying in the family. Dr. Paul Groen had been a missionary physician in Nigeria and later became a MAP board member; Dr. Steve Baker had been an RDIF recipient, and Dr. Rich Dominquez had been a MAP donor.

"We want to buy your building," they said. "You get an appraisal from a firm in Chicago, and we'll pay the appraisal price without any negotiation. We also will hire an attorney to handle the details of the transaction. You select the law firm and we will instruct them that if there are any decisions that need to be made to always come down in MAP's favor." So John Veselius, who had handled legal matters for MAP for a number of years, handled the transaction.

This was MAP's first big investment and with land and a building of our own, we finally had something of real, tangible value. Consolidating our office and warehouse space meant I no longer was spending so much time driving between locations, and with the new warehouse we were able to exercise much better control over our inventory. Having our own facility also opened the door for us to begin manufacturing some of the medicines that were not always available as donations. It was a great time in the life of the organization, and in many ways, I felt it was the beginning of MAP becoming a real family.

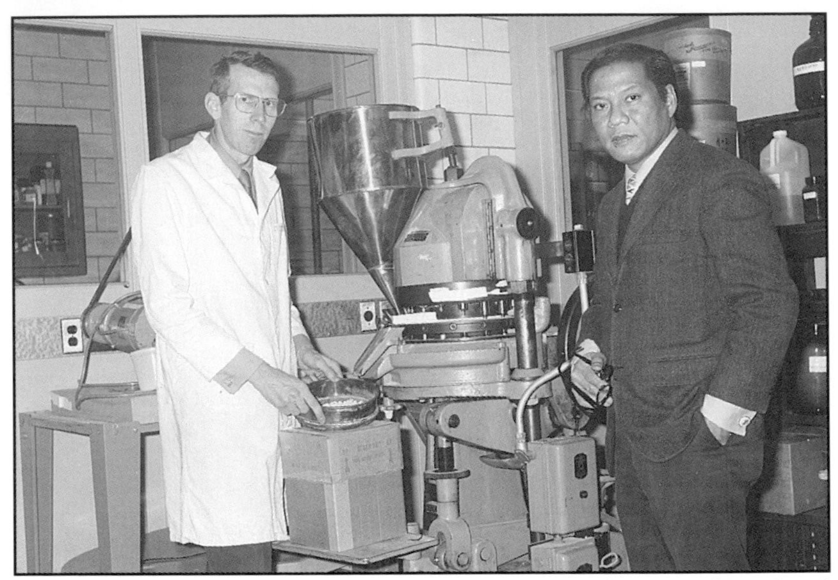

Donald Stillwell, R.Ph., with Sudan Inland Missions in Ethiopia, and Dr. Angel Arambulo inspect "green aspirin," ca. 1971.

Chapter Sixteen

Green Aspirin

Wheaton, Illinois, 1968

Certain medicines are always in high demand overseas. Antibiotics and aspirin are just two examples. Since MAP could never dictate how much a company might give, or when MAP would receive it, there have often been times when there just wasn't enough on hand to meet the demand.

One answer, in the early days of MAP, was to manufacture our own medicines. Since the supplies we shipped were for export and therefore fell outside the regulatory domain of the US Food and Drug Administration (FDA) in the late 60s, we were able to set up our own manufacturing facility to help meet the needs.

By March of 1968, MAP International was operating a manufacturing facility producing two items that were always in high demand all over the world—aspirin and tuberculosis medications.

At that time, tuberculosis had basically been eradicated in the United States, and most pharmaceutical companies weren't producing tuberculosis medicines. Since the medicines weren't being manufactured, we not only couldn't get them donated, we couldn't buy them either.

But it turned out that manufacturing our own medicines was cheaper than buying them. In a tablet, the active ingredient is only about one-tenth of what goes into a pill. The rest of what makes up the pill is primarily material used to hold it together, in a size that a person can swallow. It's amazingly simple once you break down all the parts. The only costly aspect is the labor involved.

Once we'd decided that manufacturing was the answer, we faced the question of where to begin. Since MAP was not a pharmaceutical manufacturer, we didn't have a production specialist on staff. But once again, the Lord provided the people we needed at just the right time.

John Street was a member of First Baptist Church in Wheaton. John was a pharmacist who had recently retired from a manufacturing position with a large company and moved to the Wheaton area. When a mutual friend told us about John, we invited him to our offices and told him our dream of manufacturing medicines for use overseas. John quickly signed on with the project and soon set up the production line for us.

Next, we recruited a missionary pharmacist from Ethiopia, Don Stillwell, to oversee the manufacturing process. Over the course of his service with MAP, Don earned a master's degree in manufacturing from the University of Illinois. Under Don's guidance we manufactured Pepperrazine, a tuberculosis medication, in addition to colored aspirin.

Colored aspirin was exactly that: aspirin made in various colors. The doctors and hospitals we were serving overseas thought this was a fantastic idea. Aspirin is a wonderfully effective medicine overseas, but colored aspirin was almost never available to MAP. The physicians wanted colored aspirin because it was very helpful in encouraging patients to follow through with a course of treatment.

In many contexts in the developing world, if a physician gives a patient white aspirin on the first occasion of treatment, then administers a green aspirin the next time, the impression the patient receives of being treated with different medications often has a very positive effect on the success of the treatment.

It turned out that MAP-manufactured colored aspirin and tuberculosis drugs were extremely well received. I think everyone we served was very pleased with the supplies we made.

During the time we operated our production facility, Morrel Dixon, Larry Dixon's father, became our chief technician after being trained by John Street.

Eventually, with an expanding field of responsibility for the FDA, new regulations came into effect, which prevented MAP from acting as a manufacturing agent, even for export purposes. In order to keep providing the mission hospitals overseas with the supplies they needed, we moved the entire operation to the Dominican Republic. Howard Shoemake set up a manufacturing facility there which continued to provide medicines to mission hospitals for a number of years.

MAP's stateside manufacturing facility was a short-lived episode in our history, lasting only a couple of years during the late sixties in Wheaton. This effort taught us that there are many ways to creatively cope with changing circumstances. I think this ability to innovate has been one of MAP's trademarks ever since.

The sweet face of a child from the Dominican Republic.

Chapter Seventeen

One Knight in the Dominican Republic

Santo Domingo, Dominican Republic, 1968

On March 29, 1968, the government of the Dominican Republic awarded me the nation's second highest honor. At a ceremony in Santo Domingo, Pablo Jaime Vinas, Sub-Secretary of Foreign Affairs, knighted me in the Order of Christopher Columbus.

The process leading up to this honor had started almost four years earlier, in the summer of 1964. Fred Lange, a businessman and Baptist layman from Dallas, was in the Dominican Republic on business and met Howard Shoemake. Howard was a Baptist missionary of remarkable energy and enthusiasm and, at that time, was probably the most highly regarded expatriate in the country. Through his contact with Howard, Fred learned that in the Dominican Republic some 13,000 children each year were dying from dehydration due to gastroenteritis. On his return to Dallas, Fred reported to a physician friend about the desperate conditions. Soon thereafter we received a request asking whether MAP could provide some medical assistance there.

In November of 1964, I conducted an assessment trip to the Dominican Republic with Howard Shoemake, the minister of health, and a number of Dominican physicians. I had asked Dr. C. Everett Koop and Henry Harvey to go along with me.

As we traveled toward Santo Domingo from the airport along the southern coastline we passed scenes of tall palm trees and pale sandy beaches lying beside the beautiful turquoise water of the Caribbean Sea. The beauty stood in contrast to the ugliness of the fact that so many children were dying there each year.

Visiting cities, villages, medical facilities and homes, we saw the situation first-hand and learned about the problems affecting the health of Dominican children. Many mothers were ignorant about matters related to health in childbirth and childcare, and widespread unsanitary conditions made a number of illnesses almost inevitable.

Most of the physicians in the country were based in the larger cities, and most lacked the experience and equipment to deal with gastroenteritis on such a widespread level. Throughout the country there were only eighty registered nurses. Most care was being given by inadequately trained practical nurses. There was only one hospital in the country with the facilities to rehydrate babies at risk of death from dehydration. And there were no medical missionaries in the country. The last mission hospital had been closed in 1959. Dr. Koop noted that many of the babies we saw who were sick with gastroenteritis would not make it without immediate intervention.

"The biggest need is health education," Koop said. "Everything else is a stop-gap." The most urgent need was to save the hundreds of children who would die before preventive measures could take effect. We agreed that the quickest solution was to set up rehydration centers in hospitals and clinics throughout the country. The Christian Medical Society would send short-term workers to staff the facilities and MAP would provide supplies.

When our recommendation was presented to Donald Reid Cabral, acting head of the government, he received it enthusiastically. "We welcome your help," he said. "And we will fully cooperate with your director here."

Howard Shoemake whispered to me, "Ray, who is our director?"

We didn't have one yet, so I said, "I guess you are."

"Wait a minute, Ray," Howard said. "I don't think I can take on even one additional responsibility right now."

Howard went on to describe the scope of his current responsibilities. He was incredibly busy. In addition to pastoring a church and overseeing new missionaries from his denomination, Howard was working with the Dominican civil defense, the school board, and helping set up a business school with the Santiago Chamber of Commerce, the Ford Foundation and the U.S. Agency for International Development (USAID).

I recognized that all these involvements were important and demanding. Still, I found the nerve to ask Howard, "What could be more important than saving babies?" Realizing the critical nature of the situation, Howard agreed to become MAP's country director.

We began our program in conjunction with local churches, using the sanctuary as a waiting room and the Sunday School classes as examining rooms. Throughout the Dominican Republic we helped start a number of these church clinics. In Santiago, physicians set up a nursing school. In addition, the Minister of Health began revising the materials for the country's public health education efforts.

In January 1965, rehydration fluids, scalp-vein sets and other supplies and equipment from MAP began arriving in Santo Domingo. This was long before we knew about simple salt and sugar mixtures for rehydration, so we took the medical intervention route. We provided a lot of intravenous fluids and scalp-vein needle sets, and set up rehydration centers in about fifteen cities.

Nine CMS physicians and four medical students followed. The first center had been set up in the Moscoso Puello Hospital in Santo Domingo. At the dedication ceremony, President Cabral spoke and one of the CMS physicians led a devotional. It was televised and covered by all the papers.

Soon facilities were being set up in population centers throughout the country. Howard decided the protocol for setting up the clinics, and designed the process for training workers and handling the anticipated patient load. After each center was dedicated, the MAP team would stay for several days to train personnel. In three months, MAP was supplying rehydration units in twelve hospitals and the Dominican Ministry of

Health was operating another twelve. Hundreds of mothers began bringing their sick babies. During the critical months of January and February, some centers averaged treating forty-five infants per day.

Dr. Donald Johns was a CMS member and a pediatrician from Grand Rapids, Michigan, who later became a MAP board member. Don agreed to go down with a group to teach the skills needed to carry the project out. When Don got there he loved the country and people so much, and felt such sympathy for their poverty, that when he returned to the states, he came home with nothing but the clothes on his back. He had given away every other article of clothing in the town of Barajona.

As news about the effort spread, physicians throughout the area began calling Howard and identifying themselves as Christians. As a result, Howard formed the first overseas CMS chapter with twenty of these physicians. Don Johns spoke at one of these "round table" gatherings and afterward counseled until the early morning with a government official who had been in attendance that evening.

One of the Dominican physicians Howard brought to the physician's roundtable was Dr. Gladys Germosen, who was working in a tuberculosis hospital about ten miles west of Santo Domingo. Dr. Germosen came to the CMS doctors' roundtable, then attended church services, and finally, professed faith in Christ.

The last of the MAP rehydration centers were dedicated in early April 1965.

Howard had set up an event with a big entourage of twenty cars to visit ten centers and dedicate them all in one twenty-four hour period. He arranged for us to come down with the chairman of MAP's board, Martin Andrews, and dedicate the centers with government representatives along to film for television broadcast.

We started out early in the morning that day and returned late that night. At each place we stopped the people had prepared a meal for us. The most popular dish was *San Cocha de Chiva,* which is a goat stew. As we raced from town to town with sirens blaring, every place we stopped had goat stew ready for us. The government really rolled out the red carpet for us on that trip. The minister of health was with us, as well as the minister of dental health and a camera crew.

All this was just days before the war.

On April 24, 1965, revolution broke out. It was the twenty-fourth such revolution since the Dominican Republic had gained independence in 1841. On April 28, four hundred U.S. Marines, sent by President Lyndon Johnson, arrived to evacuate U.S. citizens, and on April 29, Howard's family and other missionaries were evacuated.

But Howard stayed to continue the work we had started. He called me in Wheaton and said, "Ray, we need help. What can you send?" I promised to redouble our efforts to recruit donations from the pharmaceutical industry to help meet the needs. Howard continued to respond to calls for medicines and food from hospitals and shelters, and served as a medical missionary for both sides throughout the conflict.

On May 5, seven tons of MAP supplies arrived via Navy jets. Later, thirty-one tons more were delivered to Howard's house. Throughout the summer months, and then into the next year, Howard coordinated the distribution of MAP supplies to help ease the suffering of the conflict.

By June 1966, sufficient order had returned to the country that elections were held and Joaquin Balaguer, a conservative who had become president following Trullio in 1960, was reelected with fifty-six percent of the vote. Under Balaguer's leadership, relative stability was restored to the country.

Just one month later, in July 1966, the Ozama Baptist Church in Santo Domingo began a weekday afternoon clinic with MAP supplies. By 1967, there were eight Christian medical clinics in Santo Domingo—three were Baptist, various other groups supported four, and one was the original CMS clinic in downtown Santo Domingo.

So it was that in 1968, the government of the Dominican Republic made me a Knight in the Order of Christopher Columbus. Over the years, MAP continued to provide various levels of assistance in the Dominican Republic through church-related clinics and CMS short-term teams.

Some twenty years after I received that award, Dr. Germosen was still faithfully serving the poor through Christian clinics in Santo Domingo. I may have received an honor for my contribution, but I believe that when the full story of Christian service in the Dominican Republic is written in heaven, Howard Shoemake, Don Johns, Gladys Germosen, and many others who sacrificed far more than I, will finally receive the honor they deserve. And that's as it should be.

Chapter Eighteen

The Million Dollar Luncheon

New York City, 1971

When I left the Pan Am building in New York City that day in 1971, I felt like I was walking on air. I've often said that I flew home that day, but wasn't sure whether I used an airplane.

I'd just been given a million dollars to underwrite the MAP International/Reader's Digest International Fellowship (RDIF). Beth and I had always been very interested in helping medical students get mission field experience, and RDIF was a perfect vehicle. Since its beginning in 1971, over 1,600 senior medical students have encountered a life-changing experience through the RDIF program.

It started with what many people would call a "chance" meeting at the famous Stonybrook School for Boys in Stonybrook, New York. I don't believe in "chance" or coincidental occurrences. I believe in an almighty God who sovereignly directs the course of events so as to infallibly bring about His will for the good of His people. The letters in the word "C.H.A.N.C.E." make a good acronym to help me remember the truth: *Clearly, heaven allows no coincidental events.*

Dr. C. Everett Koop, a MAP board member, was on the Stonybrook school board, and it happened that DeWitt Wallace, the founder of *The Reader's Digest*, was visiting this particular board meeting. As God would have it, Dr. Koop and Mr. Wallace got to know each other.

When Dr. Koop found an opportunity to tell Mr. Wallace about what MAP was doing through the Short Term Missionary Program, and about the opportunity for a scholarship program, Mr. Wallace replied, "I'm very interested in that myself. I think we ought to have an article in *The Reader's Digest* about your work."

A remark like that from someone as influential as DeWitt Wallace can quickly set the wheels in motion. As soon as Koop could contact me he said, "Ray, I've got a date for you as soon as you can get to New York. On your next trip, call ahead and make an appointment to see Mr. Wallace at Reader's Digest. He wants to talk to you."

As quickly as I could, I found an excuse to be in New York, called Mr. Wallace's office, and made an appointment with him. We met in a very posh club in downtown New York, up at the top of the Pan Am building.

I arrived and met this very cordial, very grandfatherly-looking man. I can say that about Mr. Wallace now, because now I'm very grandfatherly-looking myself. I just hope I'm as cordial to others as Mr. Wallace was to me. We had a delightful lunch, and I had ample opportunity to tell him all about what MAP was doing. While we talked, Mr. Wallace said, "I want to do an article in the *Digest* about your work."

I was thrilled. *The Digest* had a circulation in the millions. An article in that magazine would provide the best exposure and publicity we could hope for.

We began to discuss who might write such an article, and Mr. Wallace, in his cordial way, asked me whether there was anyone I would particularly like to have write it. He mentioned some possibilities. One of them was Clarence Hall. Clarence had been a well known writer on the editorial staff of the *Digest* and, by this time, was retired and living in Florida. Previously, Clarence had been the Editor of the Salvation Army magazine, *War Cry.* I knew that Clarence would not only do an excellent job on the article, but he would also be sympathetic to our spiritual interests.

When I mentioned my preference for having Clarence write the article, Mr. Wallace said, "I think I can make it exciting enough for Clarence to come out of retirement and do your story." And that's exactly what he did.

Clarence spent several days with us and then wrote an article called "They Take Vacations for Humanity," focusing on MAP's Short Term Mission Program. The article appeared in the April 1971 issue.

All this was agreed over lunch with Mr. Wallace that April afternoon. Later, as we were walking out of the club, Mr. Wallace said "I understand you are interested in sending medical students overseas."

"Yes, sir. Very much." I said.

"I'd like to have a part in that," he said. "I'll see what I can do financially."

After that I flew home, so excited that I wasn't sure whether I was on a plane or not.

Mr. Wallace was a very organized man and by all the evidence he went directly to his office and made out two checks. One was from a household account and the other was from a petty cash fund. Together they totaled one million dollars. Along with the contribution, Mr. Wallace set up a committee to oversee use of the funds.

The man appointed chairman of the committee was a *Reader's Digest* employee whom I knew personally. Bill Hetherington had been one of the managing editors of the American Medical Association (AMA) publication, *Today's Health*, based in Chicago. Through my own work with the AMA, I had gotten to know Bill, and Bill had since become a sales rep for *Reader's Digest* in Chicago. As Chairman of the committee, Bill had oversight of the guidelines we laid out, which are still being followed in the RDIF program.

It was a beautiful arrangement for MAP and now, over 30 years later, some 1,600 students have benefited from that fund. Many of the students who have benefited from our various short-term programs stand out in our memory, but I'll mention one in particular, a young man named Phil Littleford.

Phil went to the Congo to work with Paul Carlson, a missionary physician who was murdered during an uprising while Phil was there. Later on, Paul's family and some of the rest of us started The Paul Carlson Foundation in his memory, to carry on Paul's work in the Ubangi area of Congo.

I have a book written by Paul's wife, Lois, entitled, *Monganga Paul: The Congo Ministry and Martyrdom of Paul Carlson, M.D.* She signed my copy with these words, "With my pleasant memories of past associations and looking forward with plans for the Paul Carlson Foundation. I'm sure these pages in this book will bring many familiar scenes. Also, may you more fully understand the medical work in Congo, Paul's love for the Congolese, and some of his dreams, Lois."

On the last page of her book, Lois wrote that some would say it was chance that brought Paul's death, chance that caused Dr. Warren Berggren to become ill and return home, thereby bringing to Congo Philip Littleford, a medical student on an RDIF fellowship under Paul Carlson's sponsorship. But she concludes, "No, not by chance. I have peace in this assurance."

I agree. And it was not by chance that MAP was formed, not by chance that DeWitt Wallace saw the value in medical student fellowships, and not by chance that RDIF has played an important role in the lives of 1,600 young women and men who have served under that fellowship. Remember the "C.H.A.N.C.E." acronym I mentioned earlier? "Clearly, heaven allows no coincidental events."

Chapter Nineteen

The Bangladesh Brigade

Bangladesh, 1971

On February 19, 1971, in Dhaka, the capital city of Bangladesh, I met with the prime minister, Sheik Mujibur Rahman, together with Dr.Viggo Olsen, a close friend and the medical director of Memorial Christian Hospital in the Chittagong District. Sheik Rahman railed against the Pakistanis.

"The barbarous Pakistani army has destroyed our economy, our hospitals, our food. They destroyed three million people and thirty million homes. We need food. We need medicine. And with the monsoon coming, we need shelter." At least the priorities were clear from the beginning: medicine, food, and shelter.

Bangladesh was the larger and more densely populated part of Bengal, the remainder of which constituted the neighboring Indian state of West Bengal. British rule in the region lasted from the eighteenth century until 1947, when East Bengal became part of Pakistan.

In 1971, reacting to West Pakistani domination, the Awani League, formed by Mujibur Rahman to fight for the autonomy of East Bengal, won control of the National Assembly. Riots broke out. Assembly sessions were postponed. Pakistani troops attacked on March 25 and on March 26, 1971, the people of East Pakistan Province declared their independence as the nation of Bangladesh (Bengali for "Bengal nation").

In the ensuing civil war, one million people died, and ten million fled to India. The independence of Bangladesh was settled on December 16, 1971, when Pakistani troops in the region surrendered to a joint force of Bangladeshi and Indian troops, but the tiny country was decimated. The new nation's first government was formed in January 1972 under Mujibur Rahman's leadership. Mujib, as he was called, became prime minister, faced with the formidable task of rebuilding a war-ravaged nation while managing the influx of ten million returning refugees.

Viggo and I embarked on a two-week survey of emergency needs in Bangladesh. Dr. Olsen was a pioneer medical missionary in Bangladesh, who was accorded almost diplomatic status and respect after long years of service to the Bengali people. Prime Minister Rahman had personally implored us to do all we could to supply food and medicine, and it was abundantly clear that housing was desperately needed for the people to survive the coming monsoon.

With the approval of the Viggo's mission board, the Association of Baptists for World Evangelism, Dr. Olsen became MAP's acting medical director. Together, Viggo and I brainstormed a solution and organized an effort that became known as "The Bangladesh Brigade."

In his book, *Daktar: Diplomat in Bangladesh*, Viggo wrote: "March 1972 was a whopping big month. On March 1 we had only a deep desire to help the stricken people of Bangladesh—but no method, no manpower, and no money! I reached Dhaka on March 31 with twenty-one colleagues and more manpower to follow, as well as grant of hundreds of thousands of dollars. Thank you, Father."

During the first week of March, Viggo and I had spent long hours planning, budgeting and putting a proposal on paper. In keeping with the results of our survey and meeting with Prime Minister Rahman, our plan included the supply of medicines and food, and the construction of four thousand houses.

Congress had approved the allocation of millions in foreign aid dollars for Bangladesh. Since MAP was registered with the

United States Agency for International Development (USAID) as a voluntary relief organization, we were able to receive a grant for nine hundred thousand dollars.

The Brigade was composed of twenty-four people, made up primarily of Wheaton College students, together with two nurses, a doctor, and a mechanic from Walnut Ridge Baptist Church in Iowa. Amazingly, in ten weeks, from March 31 through the first part of June, this team supervised the construction of 6,500 thatch-bamboo homes and repaired 3,250 others.

As the team was preparing to leave Bangladesh they were invited to a meeting with the American ambassador. The ambassador congratulated Dr. Olsen and the team, confessing that in the beginning he had tried to block the project in every way possible.

"I knew certain elements in the country surely would claim you were all CIA agents, causing me no end of trouble," the ambassador explained. "And I was sure I would receive outraged reports about miniskirts in mosques. I owe you an apology. Nothing that I feared happened. Not only did you achieve your goal, you far surpassed it. What you have done is a remarkable victory for America and for our foreign aid program in Bangladesh. I not only offer you my apology, I want to congratulate you on your marvelous work. I am proud of you, and your country is proud of you."

Building homes was only one phase of a five-part MAP program in that country. Others included providing 650 hospital beds, supplying more than $1 million in medicines and providing tons of food as well as household utensils for people who had been looted or had lost all their belongings as refugees.

Along with Viggo, I pondered the question of the ambassador's opposition to our project. He was a levelheaded, experienced man, very familiar with the country and the pitfalls of working there. Why did his expectations of disaster fail to materialize? I think Viggo summarized the answer very well.

"Our success was due to the double dedication of the Bangladesh Brigade," Viggo said. "Because our young men and women were deeply dedicated to Christ, they gained an outstanding dedication to the task to which the Lord had called them. The ambassador had no way to know that our group possessed this extra spiritual dimension that so powerfully reinforced their dedication to the work. But on the front lines it spelled the difference between failure and success."

Chapter Twenty

S.K.I.P.

India, 1971

By the early 70s it was becoming increasingly difficult for foreign missionaries to obtain the visas needed to serve in India. Many of the former mission hospitals were being nationalized and run by Indian staff. There was a great need for an organization that could help with the transition.

With the help of Ray Windsor of Bible Medical Missionary Fellowship, a cardiac surgeon from New Zealand who was a missionary in India, MAP formed the Emmanuel Hospital Association with Dr. Howard Searle as our first director.

In 1971, Beth and I were in Delhi with Howard, who was accompanying us on a visit to Landhour Christian Hospital. Landhour was located at Mussoorie, an old British field station atop a mountain in Haryana State, north of Dehli. Mussoorie had been one of the prime resorts during the days of British rule when government officials would use these "hill stations" in the hot season as an escape from the low country furnace. For some time, MAP had been providing Landhour with medicines and supplies, and there were a number of Christian doctors and nurses stationed there whom we knew.

Howard had hired a driver to take Beth and me up the rustic but incredibly beautiful road to the top of the mountain. Along the way we saw the first "ambulatory ambulance" we had ever seen—an ambulance on foot.

A woman was being carried to the hospital by a man bearing a carrier with a strap that rested against the front of his head and a basket for carrying a load on his back. This woman, obviously very ill and possibly near death, was riding all the way up the mountain in this "backpack." The lengths that suffering people would go to for treatment at Landhour was a testimony to the quality of care being provided there.

Many of the hospitals served by missions in India were providing excellent care, but most were in very rural places where public schools were generally non-existent. Although there were physicians willing to serve in those rural stations, a major obstacle was their need to provide education for their children. The most obvious answer was to send the children to boarding school, but the lack of finances needed to do that presented a big obstacle.

After we toured the hospital and had lunch with the staff, we brainstormed with Howard, trying to come up with a way to help these doctors provide the education their children needed. But we couldn't seem to come up with any workable solutions.

The problem was that we couldn't send money directly to physicians in India because of the Indian government's currency control laws.

Eventually Howard suggested a process. MAP could send medicines to the various hospitals of the Emmanuel Hospital Association. The hospitals would then owe MAP a participation share, but instead of converting rupees into dollars and forwarding them to the U.S., they would send the participation share to the EHA office in rupees. EHA could retain the rupees for the scholarship fund, and MAP could then raise funds in the U.S. to be applied against that hospital's account. The bookkeeping could get a bit complicated, but would enable us to help these physicians educate their children while avoiding the difficulties of exchanging funds between America and India.

Once we had worked out this process, the next question was what to call the program. The name we finally came up with was S.K.I.P., which stood for Scholarships for Kids of International Physicians. We felt that the name was a perfect fit for the program because it immediately put the focus of the program on children.

As we discussed possible avenues for funding this effort, Beth suggested that she could approach the Cook County Medical Society women's group to raise funds. That way we wouldn't be delving into the funds that were already being given to MAP, and possibly we would find new donors who were interested in a new kind of project.

When we got back to the states, Beth met with the director of women's programs for the American Medical Association. The director thought it sounded like a project their members would be interested in. "We're very interested in the education of doctors' children," she said. "I'll talk with a few of our groups and see if we can raise some funds."

It started in Cook County, Illinois, but soon there were some county associations in Ohio and Arkansas that were also very supportive. For many years, these groups were the sole support of the S.K.I.P. program. The doctors would send us pictures of their children, and we would forward them to the people who were supporting them. Often the supporters would write letters back to the families. One physician's family in the US adopted a physician's family in India and educated the children all the way through college.

Sadly, a time came when many of the county medical societies found other priorities consuming their energies. Soon after these support sources ended, the S.K.I.P. program ended as well.

On our visit to Landhour, Beth and I nearly met our end as well. As we made our way down the mountain, we soon realized that if the "ambulatory ambulance" passenger we'd seen was near death on the way up the mountain, we were just as near death on the way down.

Apparently, our driver had gotten hold of a bottle of moonshine. We had been there for several hours, and evidently he had quite a bit of it.

This fellow was driving down the mountain so fast that we were all terrified. The road was just one lane with some wide places where you could pass a truck or car, but otherwise it was just one lane. At the edge of the road there was a drop of two or three thousand feet before anything would stop you. There were no guard rails, just a cliff on one side and a sheer mountain face on the other.

Howard told the fellow to slow down, but that only seemed to irritate him and spur him to drive faster. He seemed to be thinking, "I'm the driver, and you can't tell me how to drive this car."

Whatever he was thinking, he didn't slow down. At one point there was a truck coming toward us. Rather than slow down, our driver whipped our car out around the truck and then around another car in front of the truck. I think we only survived by the narrowest of margins.

That was the last straw for Howard who shouted at the driver, "Stop this car NOW!" He then made the driver get out, and Howard drove the rest of the way. I suppose the driver lost face, but at least we survived.

Beth and I have often wished that the S.K.I.P. program could have survived as well. Through this unique program, MAP was able to make it possible for many physician families in India to remain in a place of vital service to the poor, while ensuring that their children received a quality education. Looking back on it now, I feel that the contribution MAP made to the families of these physicians was more than matched by the quality of care they provided for many of India's poorest people.

Chapter Twenty-One

God Builds a Team

Wheaton, Illinois, 1974

During 1974, both Beth and I spent a good bit of time in Washington collecting volumes of information on obtaining government grants. We came back with briefcases full of applications, forms, and guidelines for preparing a development grant proposal. But we just sat there, staring at the pile of paper we had accumulated and said, "Where on earth do we start?"

Sitting together in my office in MAP's new building in Wheaton in 1968, Beth and I had expressed our desire to see MAP engaged in development work for the first time. It had been clear to us for some time that meeting the needs of people in the developing world involved nutrition and community development. But we didn't have any money to start a new program. So it was that in 1974 we were looking for funding in Washington, D.C. although neither of us had ever written a grant proposal before.

The guidelines we received gave strict specifications for the proposal with work plans, budgets and additional documentation, all of which had to be prepared in multiple copes and submitted well in advance of the date when the funding would be needed. We were more than swamped—we were overwhelmed. We needed a project director. We prayed for the Lord to open a door.

Then, we had a call from Ed Morgan at the headquarters of ServiceMaster, one of the leading franchise operations in the United States in household and industrial cleaning.

"I have a man over here who I think could do more for you than he ever could working for ServiceMaster," Ed said. "We could use him, but I really feel that he would be better fitted to work with you. He's very capable, with a lot of international experience. I think you should talk to him."

"Send him over," I said. "We'll be glad to talk to him."

Bill Senn came to our office for the first time, and Beth had him fill out an application. She noticed immediately that Bill had been overseas and had worked for the U.S. government in Chile. He had also worked for UMCOR (United Methodist Committee on Relief.)

In addition, Bill and his wife, Hope, had worked in Greece and Uganda. His last job had been in a government contract in Uganda working on a rural electrification project. Clearly, he could bring a broad base of experience that would benefit MAP greatly.

At the end of Bill's interview with Beth, he bowed his head over her desk, and said, "Beth, I just have to come to work for you. I can write that grant. I can do all that." Beth later told me that with tears welling up in his eyes, Bill had said, "I just feel like this is the place where I ought to be."

"Well, the next step is to be interviewed by Ray," Beth said. "I don't make final decisions on top management."

When I interviewed Bill, I got the same positive impression Beth had received. Bill was eager to come on staff with MAP, and he had already reviewed the proposal guidelines and application papers we'd received.

"Ray, I've written lots of government grants," he said. "You don't have to worry about any of this. I understand this process because these are the same forms we used at UMCOR."

I said, "Bill, the problem right now is that I *can't* hire you. We don't have any money, and there is no way I can pay you what you need to live on." Bill and his wife Hope had three children at home. They had just moved to the Wheaton area and were living on a hand-to-mouth basis at the time.

"Eventually there would be money in the grant for a project director," I told Bill. "But from the time we start to write the proposal until we get the grant will be several weeks, if not months. Right now, I don't have the money, and I can't borrow it. If you want the job, those are the conditions you have to take it on."

And Bill said, "Okay, I'll take it."

So Bill came to MAP and worked for several months without any salary. Everyone in the office and at church helped as much as they could, but Bill's family really struggled to make ends meet. Yet they managed to survive while Bill put the grant proposal together.

In response to Bill's proposal, USAID approved a $1.1 million dollar grant for expanding MAP's community health projects in the developing countries of Ecuador, Bolivia, Haiti, Guatemala, Bangladesh, India, Uganda, Zaire and West Africa. That same year MAP established its first regional office in Quito, Ecuador. This was MAP's first major operating grant from a government agency, designed to encourage organizational development. Ultimately it led to all of the community health work MAP later did.

Bill began assembling a team that could carry out all that we had committed to do. The ensuing process brought us some of the greatest assurance we've ever had of God's leading in hiring new staff.

Jack Robinson was one of Bill's first recruits. Jack was a professor at a French-language seminary in Banqui, Zaire. Jack had started college as a pre-med student but felt the Lord redirecting him along the way. His fluency in French was a perfect fit for a role in our emerging community development program.

Then the next staffer we needed was a program evaluator. The grant required the individual to have professional qualifications.

On a trip to West Africa I stopped off at ELWA Hospital in Liberia to see Bob Schindler, a missionary physician who later became a MAP board member.

ELWA was a short-wave radio station run by Sudan Interior Mission. The call-sign letters "ELWA" were simply the ones given to the station when they applied for their transmitter license, but the group soon came up with a name that gave sense to the acronym. They identified their station as "Eternal Love Winning Africa," although they have since gone on to broadcast all over the world.

Ever the innovator and pioneer, Bob had recognized an opportunity and started a hospital in connection with the radio station. Bob, a CMS board member, brought a wealth of missionary experience to the table, along with proven ability in training students, as well as the fact that he stayed current in his field. At this writing, Bob is president of The International Association of Christian Physicians and directs the COIMEA (Committee on International Medical Educational Affairs) program for CMS, recruiting specialists from various disciplines to lecture at medical schools overseas. (CMS has since changed its acronym to CMDS, the Christian Medical and Dental Society, and now to CMDA, standing for Christian Medical and Dental Association.)

As always, the first thing Bob wanted to know about was the most current project I was working on. "I'm looking for the proverbial needle in a haystack," I said. "We need someone with professional credentials to fill an important slot – a strong believer with planning skills, who meets the professional program evaluator requirement."

To my surprise Bob said, "You know, I think we've got a person on our staff at the radio station who might be interested."

At the radio station I met Don Miller. It turned out that Don had a Ph.D. from Michigan State where he had studied under Ted Ward as a program evaluator. When I saw his resume, I realized he matched up perfectly. Don brought a new degree of professionalism to our staff and he was always challenging our thinking to go beyond what we believed was possible in purely human terms.

Some might describe the way we put this team together as "happenstance." But I didn't go to ELWA looking for Don Miller. And Don wasn't there to wait for my visit. I believe that the Lord orchestrated MAP's need and Don's presence, as well as all the other staffers we recruited for this team.

Once the team was assembled, their first efforts were in community development in South America. Being fluent in

Spanish and very familiar with South America, Bill ultimately opened the door for all of MAP's work in Latin America.

Arriving in Guatemala after the 1976 earthquake, Bill initiated a water project, a home rebuilding project, and various agriculture and craft projects. We distributed health-training materials and taught women how to develop sewing into cottage industry tailoring businesses.

To help with the reconstruction of homes lost in the earthquake, Bill designed a house that was earthquake-proof. To accomplish that, a house has to be either extremely rigid or extremely flexible. Bill and an engineer he recruited designed a reinforced-frame house made with cement block that proved to be invulnerable to the tremors common to the area.

At one time, we envisioned building a small hospital in the area of Guatemala where we worked. Although it wasn't to be in our time there, Wycliffe has since located a small medical facility there, giving us the feeling that the vision has been fulfilled even if we were not the ones God used to bring it to fruition.

Eventually, the Guatemalan government made the determination that they couldn't guarantee the safety of foreigners living in such a rural area. Bill and Hope had to cut their ties with the ministry there and be reassigned to other duties. I think when Bill and Hope left that community; they left a part of their heart there. They both felt so very much a part of that community.

Beth and I have always believed that Bill and Hope Senn were God-sent to MAP's work in community development. Bill always seemed to know just which way to go, and there was never any hesitation in his decisions. Bill was exactly the right person for that grant, and Hope was a perfect match for him. Bill is retired now, and Hope has gone on to be with the Lord. We miss them both.

Health education is an ongoing process in Africa.

Chapter Twenty-Two

MAP in Southern Sudan

Sudan, 1974

At a village in Sudan called Akot there was a small medical facility run by the staff of ACROSS, which is an acronym for the African Committee for the Rehabilitation of Southern Sudan. Beth and I had flown there with our MAF pilot, Bob. Before landing, we flew low over a rudimentary airstrip that had been hacked out of the jungle. Bob didn't like what he saw. He pulled up and cir cled the area, finding that the closest airstrip within driving distance of Akot was a four-hour drive away.

"Ray, there is no way we can land that far away. Get some-one to come with a jeep, make the trek back, and do it in a day," Bob said. "But one day is all the time we've got."

"What are we going to do?" I asked.

"This is where we break the rule," Bob said.

"What rule?" I asked. I've since learned that one of MAF's most strictly held rules is this—never land on a jungle airstrip until it has been walked by someone from MAF.

"I'll drop down so we can buzz the airstrip," Bob said. "I'll eyeball it on my side and you check it out on the other side. Let me know if you see any big holes. Then we'll see about landing there."

I said, "Okay," and we circled to make another approach and buzzed the runway at an altitude of about 10 feet. By that time, the noise of the plane had drawn the whole village out.

The next time around Bob said, "Okay, this time I'm going to try it low enough to gently touch the landing gear on the runway. We'll cover the length of the runway like that and see how it feels." Then he added, "You keep a close watch on your side."

All this time, Beth was in the back of the little plane, praying.

We skimmed the runway once over lightly and it seemed safe enough. "I think we can make it," Bob said.

The word "think," made me a little uncomfortable, but we circled again and this time sat it down for a landing. By this time the entire village was out, along with the ACROSS workers. I have tremendous confidence and respect for MAF's pilots, but that was one time I was glad to get my feet on the ground at one of the ACROSS stations in Sudan.

In 1972 a group of executives from non-governmental organizations and missions including Africa Inland Mission, the Episcopal Church, TEAR Fund, CBM, World Vision, and MAP met at the airport in Newark, New Jersey. Our objective was to come up with a way to address an emerging opportunity for service in Sudan.

Sudan had been closed to missionary work for a long time. But in 1972, Gaafar Muhammad al-Nimeiry became Sudan's first elected president. Nimeiry signed a peace treaty with Ethiopia's government in Khartoum called the Ethiopian Accord. Nimeiry was working to consolidate his power, and we all hoped the situation would open the door long enough for us to develop a program in Sudan to help address some of the desperate needs there.

As a result of that meeting, by 1974, we had established ACROSS and opened an office in Nairobi, Kenya to oversee the work in Sudan. We had started a number of schools, health facilities, and agriculture projects, as well as cooperating in some work with Bible colleges and seminaries.

One of the cooperating organizations in ACROSS was the British MAF. This was a vital partnership because of the difficulty of getting around on the ground in that part of Africa. The MAF plane made a regular circuit called the milk run and they would deliver mail, fresh produce and eggs. We would make our deliveries in a village, have supper, spend the night, and then go on the next day. It was on one of these trips that Beth was introduced to bats and the "bush shower."

By the time we arrived at Akot, we had been in the bush for a long time. Beth said, "If there is any way to arrange it, I really would like to have a shower." Our host said he would see what he could do and went about setting up a little shed. When they were finished they called Beth over and announced, "Okay, there's your shower stall."

There was a little girl with a bucket on the top of the shower stall. The bucket had holes in the bottom to make the shower. Beth got in the shower and the girl stood up and poured water over Beth's head. That was the first time Beth ever had that kind of a shower, and we believe it was the first time that little girl had seen a white woman.

Conditions on these trips were often *rustic* to say the least. On one trip into Sudan with Tony Atkins and a British pilot, we slept at a place out on Longbeam, in a missionary compound on the Nile River. In the little hut where we stayed we had to take care to sleep away from the wall because bats were covering the ceiling, and bat droppings were covering the walls. That experience, however, wasn't nearly as harrowing as the time in Juba, the capital of Sudan, when Beth was rooming with one of the young women serving there as a volunteer. It was just one room actually a shed where the young lady was staying. Inside the shed were two beds and the few necessities the young woman had brought with her. There were windows on each side of the hut and another up over the bed. Screens covered the windows, and the hut entrance had a screen door. The bathroom was in a little outhouse in back.

At bedtime Beth's roommate said, "Now, don't worry, but there are bats up in the top of this shed. If you don't bother them, they won't bother you, and everything will be fine." I'm pretty sure Beth didn't have any intention of bothering the bats.

They went to bed and later that night, in the dark, bats began to flutter down and cling to the screens over the windows. Beth had never seen a bat up close before. To her, they were the most ugly things she had ever seen. It was bad enough to have them up in the ceiling, much less to have them fluttering down around the windows. She took one look at them and covered up with the sheet for the rest of the night. Beth would stick her head out every once in a while to see if they were still there. I'm afraid Beth didn't get much sleep that night.

The situations we encountered on these trips ranged from the humorous to the dangerous. On one of the milk runs, Beth held a carton of eggs in her lap throughout the trip. Each time we landed, we'd lose a couple of eggs. That was no great loss, but it made us all the more concerned whenever we carried cargo that was fragile or dangerous.

On one trip, we had picked up vials of blood samples, which we were transporting out of the country to have tested. There was fear that hemorrhagic fever had been responsible in the deaths of several the ACROSS staff.

Years before, a type of hemorrhagic fever had been discovered in the town of Lassa, Nigeria. Jeanette Troup, one of the medical missionaries with SIM in Lassa had died of hemorrhagic fever, and it had become known as Lassa fever. I believe it is still referred to by that name in some medical journals. We were so afraid that if anything happened to that plane, all of us would have contracted the fever. Up in the nose of the plane we had numerous vials of blood that we were taking out of the country for testing.

An unusual occurrence near the end of this trip had some effects that have stayed with us ever since.

We returned to Nairobi with Jack and Jodie Hough who were staying in the hotel with us, along with a young man named Tony Neeves. Tony was a photographer for TEAR Fund, a Christian agency based in Great Britain, who had been covering the trip and was stopping over on his way out of the country.

I had first met Tony in Bangladesh, but Beth had gotten to know him for the first time on this trip. Throughout our travels, the two of them sat together and talked at every opportunity. Tony's mother—"Mum" as he called her—had died not long before. As he shared his story with Beth, she began to feel a bond with this young man who was so much like a son of her own.

After arriving in Nairobi, we went out to dinner. When we came back to the hotel there was a bouquet of flowers from Tony. Later that night, he dropped by to say good-bye because he was leaving the next morning.

As we talked, Tony mentioned that he had felt very lonesome since his mother had died. He went on for some time about how he was feeling. Suddenly, in a flash of inspiration, Beth said, "Tony, are you looking for a Mother? Do you want me to be your Mum?"

Tony was surprised for a moment, and then said, "Would you?"

Beth said, "Oh, yes. I'd love to be your second mother." And from that time on, we have been very close to Tony and his family.

Down through the years we have stayed in close touch and kept each other informed about all the things that happen with our families. Tony is the director of International Development for Compassion in Europe and now lives in London. On a number of occasions Tony and his family have visited the States and stayed with us for weeks at a time. He's a very dear friend and our children have always considered him a foster family member.

Looking back on our excursions with ACROSS it's clear that despite the dangers of tricky landings or the discomforts of sleeping in bat-infested huts, we never lost anything but a little sleep. And all that we gained, especially our "foster" son Tony, was priceless by comparison.

Health care workers and patient at a medical clinic in the Middle East.

A recent street scene in Palestine.

Chapter Twenty-Three

Sheik Abut

Abu Dhabi, United Arab Emirates, 1975

In a small town called Al Ain, deep in the desert of the United Arab Emirates, the Oasis Hospital had received a special shipment of medicines.

The value of the medicines in that shipment had put MAP over the one million dollar mark in medicines we had provided to missions and hospitals overseas. Beth and I had planned an assessment trip to Al Ain to document the impact of that historic shipment.

For some time prior to this, Jerry Longjohn, the hospital administrator for The Evangelical Alliance Mission (TEAM) and Dr. Pat Kennedy, the missionary doctor, had been begging us to visit. Each time I have given them the same reply.

"We'd love to come—and we will," I said, "just as soon as someone puts in a road from the airport to the hospital!"

The hospital sat among dunes of shifting sand one hundred miles from the airport at Abu Dhabi. By this time I was too experienced a traveler to risk getting stuck in a sand dune. We were thrilled when we finally received a call from Jerry saying, "Now you can come."

As our plane touched down on the strip of black tarmac stretched across the flat sand, the rainbow of beautiful flowerbeds surrounding the airport struck both Beth and me.

Amazed that such brilliantly colored delicacies could flourish in the desert environment, we were even more amazed when further inspection revealed little plastic tubes coming up beneath each flower, feeding them with water from underground. The surprise flowerbeds would prove to be merely the first sign of the lengths to which the local sheik would go to ensure that his hometown was well appointed in every way.

A second surprise greeted us when our friend Jerry met us in a very nice Mercedes sedan. While often considered a luxury in the States, Jerry explained that Mercedes automobiles were one of the few brands that had proven durable enough to withstand the desert environment. Not only that, the Mercedes was also one of the few brands available in this desert municipality because a dealership had been established to meet the transportation needs of the local sheik.

Jerry and the Mercedes soon carried us to the edge of town, and I found that we were not only on a new road, but riding on an eight-lane, divided highway that the British would call a dual carriageway. After World War II, the Emirates had been granted autonomy by England. In 1971 Qatar and Bahrain became separate states, but a hint of the British presence still remained in this road which looked like it had been lifted whole from some other land and dropped intact to the desert floor.

The tarmac ran straight as an arrow as far as we could see, and beyond. We sailed along with no towns, no traffic, and no traffic lights. Along the way we passed a few people with camels, but that was it. Two miles outside town we crossed over a bridge. A bridge? In the desert?

"What's that for?" I asked Jerry.

"Every city worth the name has a bridge, so this is ours," he said with a smile.

"Where's the water?" I asked.

"We don't have a river here so the sheik had his engineers build a bridge, then they dug a canal from the ocean so the water would run under the bridge and look like a river. It's not completed yet," he said. "But at least we have a bridge!"

I was beginning to be curious about this sheik who planted flowers in the desert, built bridges over rivers that weren't there and laid eight-lane roads where the traffic consisted mainly of camel drivers. Jerry put the Mercedes on cruise control and we spent the rest of the drive into Al Ain catching up on old times and mutual friends.

As we approached the city, Jerry suddenly hit the brakes. As we slowed he said, "I've got to put it in four-wheel drive to get to the hospital."

I was about to ask "why" when the car dipped suddenly and the whine of tires on pavement changed to the muffled hum of tires on sand.

"Pavement ends here," Jerry said.

Just then I noticed a large, ornate building rising up along the roadside.

"That's Sheik Abut's compound," Jerry said. "He owns the whole area, and he's our benefactor. The sheik has recently bought a new x-ray machine for the hospital and sent the technician to the States for training. He's the one who asked that a hospital be established here, and of course, we were eager for the opportunity to serve. Although we treat anyone who needs our help, the sheik really wanted a hospital for the Asians, Indians, and Pakistanis who come here to work on his projects."

Again, we were amazed. Was there any more unlikely place for a mission hospital to minister to such a wide spectrum of cultures and nationalities than here in Al Ain, a hundred miles out in the desert? I'd seen the Lord work in mysterious ways before, but this was giving me a completely new perspective. The sheik might have been going out of his way to build an impressive empire, but the Lord was going even farther to build His kingdom.

After lunch at the hospital, Jerry took us to see the newest building in Al Ain—a brand new Hilton Hotel.

Passing through the entrance we encountered one of the most gorgeous foyers I have ever seen. From the lobby, a winding staircase wound around a beautiful crystal chandelier on its way up to the ballroom. The entire building was a picture of elegance.

At the front desk I asked, "How many guests do you have?"

"One," the attendant said. "One family. This is the first family we've had in a long time."

Inquiring about the rates, I learned that they were good. It would have been a great place for vacation—except for the cost of getting there.

I asked Jerry, "What is a hotel like this doing in such a forsaken place?"

"The sheik built it," he replied.

Back at the hospital, Dr. Kennedy mentioned that the sheik would soon learn that we were in town.

"You've been a great benefactor to the hospital, providing medicines and supplies," Pat said. "If you don't pay a visit to the sheik, he may be offended."

It was fall of the year, during Ramadan, and the hospital staff had planned to have a dinner in our honor at the hospital with the staff that night. It was getting close to suppertime.

"Come on," Jerry said. "We'd better rush over there and see the sheik. Just go see him, without calling ahead, so he won't be offended."

Arriving at the sheik's elaborate compound, Jerry, Pat, Beth, and I were ushered into a gigantic hall with oriental rugs on the floor two inches deep and brocade settees lining the walls. After we'd sat for a time, Jerry said, "It's taking the sheik a long time. He usually comes out right away when we visit."

Soon the sheik appeared at the far end of the hallway and announced in Arabic, "Dinner is ready." Now we knew the cause of the delay. From the time we had arrived, the sheik's servants had been preparing a dinner in our honor. Since it was Ramadan, the Islamic law required Sheik Abut and his people to fast until sundown. Now that it was past sunset, we were ushered into a dining hall.

Beth was the only woman present. The women of the sheik's harem were in another building, and Jerry felt bad that he hadn't thought to bring one of the nurses from the hospital along so Beth could go back and see the women's quarters.

We sat down at places set with huge bowls of rice and meat. Of course, they wouldn't let you serve yourself; the servants served your plate for you. The food was so good, but there was so much of it. When we were stuffed and couldn't eat another bite, the sheik commented that Beth was not eating. "She doesn't eat much," I said. But really, Beth was already stuffed and was just pushing the food around her plate because there was so much.

After a while, the sheik rose and left the room, and we were shown into another room to wait for him. More servants came in with Turkish coffee, tea, and various desserts.

While we waited, I asked Jerry, "What will they do with all those leftovers?"

"Our dinner was just the first go-round for that food," Jerry said. "Remember when you got up from your place at the table, how that little boy slid in under you? That's one of the boys from the sheik's family. When the guests are finished, they come in and eat. If there is anything left over, it will go to the women. After the women are through, it goes to the animals. That's the pecking order."

Soon the sheik came in and sat down to visit with us. To make small talk I said to the sheik, "You must be younger than I; my beard is white but yours is gray."

The sheik laughed heartily and said, "I paint mine," meaning that he dyed his beard. Then the sheik leaned over to Dr. Kennedy and said he had a breaking out in his skin. He had an irritation from the dye he was using on his beard.

So, with a straight face, Pat turned to me and said, "Ray, does MAP supply non-allergenic hair dye for sheiks in Arabia?"

"All the time," I replied with an equally straight face.

So Pat told the sheik that MAP would supply him with a special dye for his beard that would prevent the breaking out. The sheik was very grateful.

Soon we said our good-byes and headed back to the hospital to sit down at another dinner the hospital had arranged. Halfway through there was a knock at the door. One of the sheik's men had a brought sack of money and said, "This will cover any expenses you have for the dye," he said. "The sheik doesn't take anything for free." To cover the cost of providing the dye we promised, the sheik had sent us several hundred dollars worth of local currency.

Back in Wheaton, Beth asked her beautician where we could get the kind of hair dye the sheik needed. Then we sent a six-month supply to the sheik by air freight. After the sheik's people saw what it was, they found they could get it from a supplier in another Emirate. But the sheik said, "No. I don't want it from there. To be good it has to come from MAP."

So from that time until the sheik passed away, about every six months we'd send a shipment of dye to Sheik Abut. He, in turn, continued as the benefactor of the hospital, supplying the staff with new equipment, training for the nationals, and other assistance to keep the Oasis Hospital up and running.

The supplies Oasis had received from MAP, marking one million dollars in medical aid MAP had provided overseas, was a special shipment. But perhaps in the long run, the small shipments of hair dye we sent to Sheik Abut every six months were even more special. By maintaining the confidence and good will of the sheik, those shipments, though insignificant from a medical point of view, played a significant role in the long-term ministry of the Oasis Hospital.

Chapter Twenty-Four

Billy and the Earthquake

Guatemala, 1976

In 1976, a devastating earthquake hit Guatemala killing some twenty thousand people and leaving one million homeless.

This was in the period before the Billy Graham Association had developed Samaritan's Purse as the vehicle for their mercy ministries. Up to this time, MAP had done a lot of relief work in connection with Billy Graham's organization.

After the earthquake, Billy was invited to go back to Guatemala to minister, so he called me and asked me to go along.

"Ray," he said. "If I'm going into Guatemala, I want you there with me. We may need some medicines or other supplies from MAP."

"Fine, I'll meet you there," I said.

I arranged my upcoming travel schedule to meet Billy in Guatemala City. When I arrived, Billy was there, along with his photographer, Richard Busby, and a young man who was serving as the interpreter. This young man, who was destined to become well known in his own right, was Luis Palau. He has since become a renowned evangelist throughout the world.

The main focus of the visit to Guatemala was an afternoon service at the First Presbyterian Church in Guatemala City. The earthquake had left a gaping hole in the center of the church roof, and pieces of the underlying structure were exposed. Of course, after an earthquake the area frequently experiences the tremors of aftershocks. At times, these can be strong enough to register as entirely separate earthquakes. It was no different here.

When the afternoon arrived, about four hundred had gathered for the service. Billy was preaching about the power of the Holy Spirit when the aftershock hit.

I suppose these days there are plenty of people in California who can tell you what it feels like. But to a Midwesterner born and raised in Chicago, ground that undulated like the surface of the ocean was a strange feeling to say the least.

At first, there is an almost imperceptible sensation of unnatural motion and you think, "Did I just feel something move?" Then, almost immediately, you think, "I just felt the earth move."

In the amount of time it takes to register those thoughts, one of two things will have occurred— the tremor will have subsided as quickly as it came, or else you're in a full blown aftershock that can easily bring down a quake-damaged building before you've had time to move.

Standing in the back of the church with Billy's song leader, Cliff Barrows, we were able to watch the congregation transition through that entire emotional sequence. Together, we felt that first uneasy, but unmistakable, movement of the building. Then the roof seemed to heave a sigh. We could feel the tension rise in the crowd as they sensed what was happening.

A swelling movement, like the swelling of a wave before it curls and crashes down on the beach, rippled through the crowd. There was an upward surge as though the whole congregation was going to lift out of their seats in unison. But then, just as quickly, the aftershock passed. Everyone settled back in their seats and the service continued.

Later, Cliff, Luis, Busby and I were back on the plane with Billy and Ruth, headed for Mexico on our way back home. We learned that Ruth had been back at the hotel making preparations for our departure. When the aftershock hit, she had been sitting directly beneath a large chandelier in the lobby. The manager had come running over, frantic to move her away from the danger.

"Billy," I said, "What did you think about it when all those people started to get up during the service?"

"Oh," he said, "Since I was preaching on the Holy Spirit, I thought everyone there was being filled with the Spirit at that same moment."

"Are you kidding?" I said. "Didn't you feel that after-shock?"

Luis said, "I certainly felt it. I was standing there beside Billy thinking about what I would do to cover him if the rest of that ceiling started to come down on us."

But Billy didn't seem to believe it.

"No," he said. "That was the power of the preaching."

We discussed it for quite a while, trying to convince Billy that a tremor had hit in the middle of his sermon. But I don't think Billy was ever completely persuaded that the effect we all witnessed was an earthquake that happened while he was preaching.

In flight over Guatemala, Ray Knighton and the Reverend Billy Graham discuss relief efforts for the victims of the 1976 earthquake there. Ruth Graham surveys the damage below.

A shipment of medical supplies is delivered to El Salvador in 1986.

Epilogue

Wheaton, Illinois, 1980

During 1980, Russia invaded Afghanistan. In response, President Jimmy Carter instituted economic sanctions against Russia and the U.S. boycotted the Summer Olympics in Moscow. In Washington State, Mt. St. Helens erupted. In Washington, D.C. an equally seismic shift occurred as Ronald Reagan was elected president in a landslide victory, and Republicans gained control of the Senate.

In 1980, seismic changes were happening for MAP as well. On October 9, 1980, Larry Dixon and I embarked on a journey to meet with MAP partners around the world. Our departure from the States marked an important departure for Beth and me as well. After nearly 30 years with CMS and MAP, I had decided to retire.

The itinerary for this trip took Larry and me to England for meetings with the board of ACROSS, then for similar meetings with Christoffel Blindenmission (CBM) in Germany. Then it was on to India, Sri Lanka, Bangladesh, and Thailand before returning home.

On reaching my decision to retire, I had recommended Larry to fill the position of president, and the board had graciously accepted. The main objective for this trip was to establish Larry as MAP's new president in the eyes of some of our long-standing partners.

It was a blessing that while Larry himself had previously departed MAP for a time, his return to the organization had made it possible for me to consider making this move. Larry and his wife, Agnes, had moved to Raleigh, North Carolina, to be near her parents. Larry had taken a job with an agricultural equipment manufacturer and was traveling throughout the region as a representative for the company's products.

One evening, after Larry had been away from MAP for about eighteen months, Beth and I were invited to dinner at the Wheaton home of Larry's parents, Morrel and Maria Dixon. Larry and Agnes were in town for a visit. That visit with the Dixons got me thinking. Later that night I telephoned Larry at his parent's home and got straight to the point. "Larry, we need you," I said. " It's time for you to come back to MAP."

The next day, Larry called me from a pay phone. "Ray, were you serious last night?" he asked.

I assured Larry that I was very serious. I felt MAP needed his unique experience and leadership potential. When Larry left MAP he had been director of our warehouse operations. I offered him the opportunity to return and take charge of the day-to-day operations of the entire organization.

Soon after Larry was back on staff, I felt that the time had come for a change. I felt I had physically run out of gas. Intellectually, I felt as though my imagination was dry; I had run out of ideas. It wasn't until years later that we realized I was experiencing the onset of Parkinson's disease. In retrospect, it might have been sufficient if I had simply taken a sabbatical. But God was sovereign in the timing of my arrival at MAP, and I believe He sovereignly superintended this time of departure as well.

By early 1981, after some time of rest and reflection, I felt ready to answer a new call to service. Ken Taylor, the founder of Tyndale House Publishers who had written the paraphrased *Living Bible*, asked me to come aboard as assistant to Dr. Lars Dunberg, president of Living Bibles International, to help with organizational development and troubleshooting for overseas projects. After my many travels in India with MAP, it was a great thrill for me to be "introduced" as an L.B.I. staff member in India's Maharashtra State, because it coincided with the introduction of the *Living Bible* in the local "Marati" language.

Meanwhile, Larry had taken on the responsibility of leading MAP into a vigorous period of expansion and development. He brought to his role as MAP's president a deep-seated determination to improve, and his leadership forged the way for a number of initiatives that would shape the organization throughout the next twenty years in a period of exciting growth.

In 1981, computerizing MAP's inventory and distribution systems brought a new level of professionalism to the distribution of medicines and supplies around the world. By 1984, the reputation MAP had developed resulted in the Pharmaceutical Manufacturer's Association designating MAP as their agency of choice for distributing donated medicines and supplies. Fueled by civil strife and political unrest that year, a terrible famine was raging in Ethiopia. Effective relief response helped solidify MAP's reputation as a global partner in addressing critical needs, both in emergency situations and in health development. During this time, Larry also took the initial steps in the long but vital process of turning over MAP's regional offices to national leadership.

Shortly after our retirement from MAP, Beth had taken a position with World Relief, and by 1985, was working with their executive director, Jerry Ballard, as assistant to the president for administration. We received a phone call from Larry, asking Beth to come to Brunswick, Georgia, to participate in some publicity events surrounding the relocation of MAP from the Midwest to the southeastern coast. We agreed, and it was during this trip that Beth received a strong impression of God's leading for MAP to move to Brunswick as well.

MAP's move to Brunswick in 1985 gave the organization a fresh start and brought in a lot of new staff with new ideas and fresh perspectives, as we started anew in a new community.

After ten years in our new location, Larry felt that the time had come for him to move on to new challenges in the private sector, and Paul Thompson came in as president.

Paul brought an experienced professionalism to his role as MAP's president and during his short tenure from 1996 to

1999 proved to be an essential part of the transition to the future. Among Paul's most important contributions was leading MAP through a two-year process of redefining our mission, vision, and *Guiding Principles.*

Paul felt that the presence of the founders had a positive effect on both the staff and the supporters, so he took steps to get Beth and me more involved in the work of MAP and allocated an office for our use at headquarters. He also recruited a number of key board members, including Dr. David Hungerford, who is now chairman of the board. I believe that Paul's efforts, in a relatively short time-span, had a major impact in strengthening MAP's team of staff, supporters, and leadership.

Perhaps most significantly, it was Paul who placed in a leadership position a relatively young staff member who had shown a lot of potential for leadership: Michael Nyenhuis.

In 1994, Michael, previously a reporter for the Florida Times-Union in Jacksonville, Florida, had joined MAP's publications staff. As Larry departed and Paul took over, God was positioning Michael for a role with MAP that neither MAP nor Michael had foreseen. But all along, God was anticipating our needs. Upon Paul's departure in 1999, Michael was named interim president, and was unanimously appointed to the position of president and CEO in April 2000.

Michael brought an entirely new level of optimistic energy to the role of president and CEO. Together with MAP's board of directors, Michael has plotted a direction for MAP in the new millennium that shows promise of growth and expansion far beyond what we have seen in the first fifty years of the organization. Under Michael's leadership MAP implemented new, strategic directions for the medicines program, as well as developing strategic directions for community development work and the organization's highly regarded HIV/AIDS programs.

Individual development programs were implemented for current staff, and efforts were increased to recruit additional highly qualified staff for positions as they become available. Under Michael's leadership, MAP has made great strides in developing the Internet as a relationship-building communication link with the widespread network of supporters, and embarked on a new financial campaign to increase the resource base as MAP moves into the future.

As Beth and I look back over the years since MAP started in 1954, we feel that God has given us a unique privilege. We've been in a position to witness firsthand the growth of a special organization, from the earliest moments of conception, through an uncertain infancy and adolescence, to a place of experience and maturity in the world of international relief and development.

Along the way, we have seen remarkable demonstrations of the providence and sovereignty of God, and that has done more to increase our confidence and faith in God than perhaps anything else that could have happened to us.

Today, MAP has staff filling important positions around the world. We remember days when we couldn't fill important staff positions around a single room. MAP is today striving to raise several million dollars. We saw days when we couldn't raise ten dollars. If we have learned anything from the experience of those days, and the years that followed, we learned the truth of Ephesians 3:20, that God "is able to do exceeding abundantly above all that we ask or think."

In the introduction to her fabulous book, *The Hiding Place*, Corrie ten Boom writes that all the people and experiences that come into our lives are part of God's perfect preparation for a future that only He can see. As we move ahead, into this future that only God can see, we have full confidence that glorious things lie ahead for the staff, the board, and the supporters of MAP International. As someone more eloquent than I once said, "We may not know what the future holds, but we know Who holds the future."

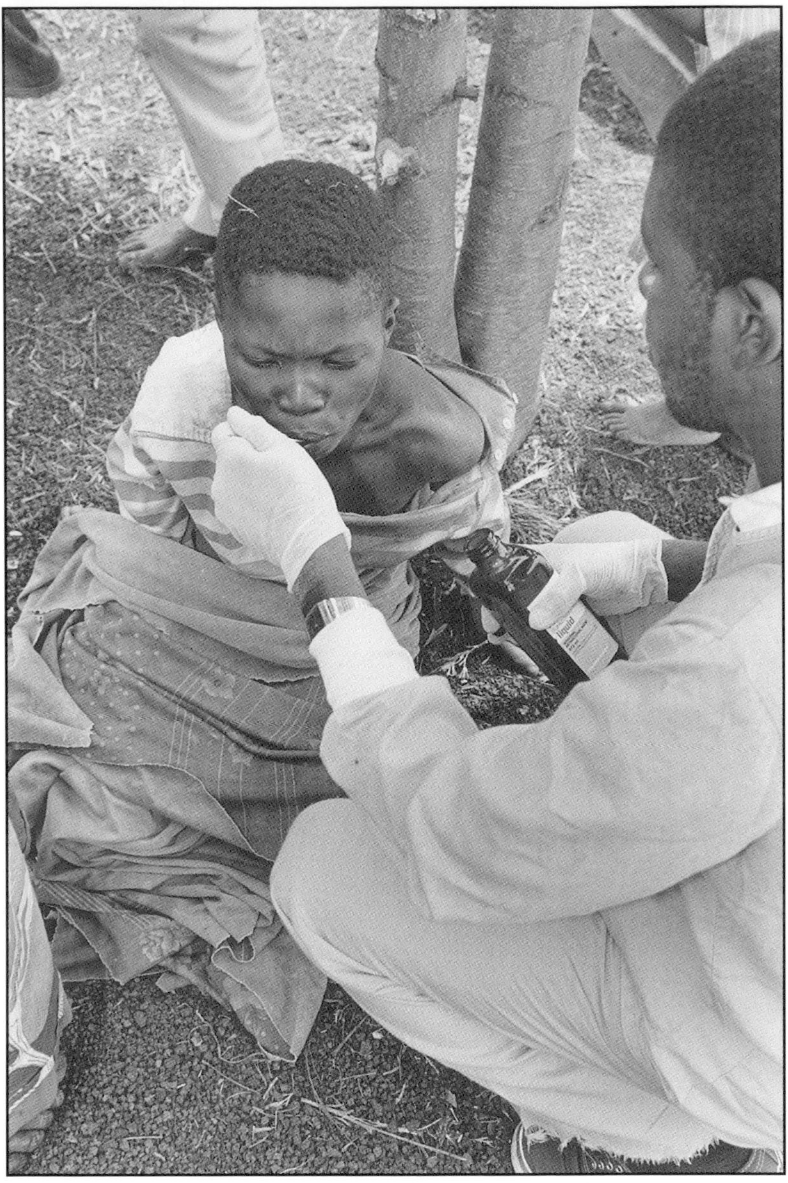

Hope "by the spoonful" in Africa, 1995.

Afterword

St. Simons Island, Georgia, 2001

Our children, Nancye Knighton Jones, David Reed Knighton, Thomas Reed Knighton and Michael Reed Knighton, are precious gifts from the Lord. Through the years, I feel that each one profited along with us—and sometimes struggled along with us—as we tried to follow God's leading in our lives, in the life of our family, and in the ministry of MAP International.

On May 29, 1992, on the occasion of our second retirement, our middle son, Tom, presented us with the following poem. Although Tom composed the poem, I feel that the sentiments it contains express the feelings of all our children, and provide a fitting afterword to the events related in this book.

To Mom and Dad
May 29, 1992

We loved it . . . we hated it
But we never doubted
Its importance

MAP

You were called
Driven to respond,

It was His plan
A cup of cold water
In His name.

The world is grateful,
I'm grateful
And proud
Of both of you.

Thanks for letting me be a part of your dream

Calling you "Ray and Beth"
Was tough at times
Life at MAP wasn't easy
But good things rarely are.
I'm profoundly changed from the experience
My worldview,
My contribution,
My dreams,

All have been shaped by
Our years together
At MAP . . .

The legacy lives on.
My boys have just connected . . .
"Do you know my Gumbah works at MAP?"
Most important
They know you help the poor
In Jesus' name.

You can retire
Confident,
That your lives have counted.
His love reflected in the faces
Of many
Through you.

This is a time for beginnings,
To refresh your vision,
To contribute
In a different way

But no less important.

We love you
And thank you
For what has been
And
For what God will continue to do

Tomorrow . . .

With our love and admiration,
Tom, Joan, Matthew, and Aaron